The Mottos

The guiding principles behind creating an enchanting

relationship and keeping your love blooming

Dr Georgina Barnett and Susie Ambrose

Acknowledgements

We would like to thank psychologists Rachel Sharpless, Lemarc Thomas and Trudy Hill for their contributions.

Additionally, we acknowledge and thank the employees at Seventy Thirty, especially Lorraine Donovan for their assistance with research for this book.

Dedication

We dedicate this book to our amazing members and coaching clients, both past and present. We feel privileged to have been part of your journey. We would also like to thank the people we love who have contributed to our insights into the world of romance.

Contents

Introduction

Part 1 – The key mottos

Part 2 – Mottos to help you prepare for your best relationship

Get an insight into your partner

Put time and thought into your relationship

What women really want

Happiness goals – are you and your partner reading from the same book?

How to keep your relationship alive

Improve emotional communication with your partner

The primary source of miscommunication in relationships

Understand the differences between how men and women communicate

Make time for love

Understand the science of love

The importance of being honest about your feelings

How to be mindful

The power of forgiveness

Introducing a new partner to your friends and family

Balancing the power in your relationship

Confession is good for the soul

Children

Age differences in a relationship

Men and their mates

'I don't love you, but I can't leave you'

Do I stay or do I leave?

Is religion a big deal?

Deciding whether or not to have children

Becoming a step-parent

Introducing your child to your new partner

Dating when you both have children

Stress over Christmas

Part 5 – Mottos to help you invest in yourself and your relationship

Keep working on your self-esteem

Why do women check out other women?

How to maintain good mental health

Self-image, confidence and success

How to adopt a positive mindset

Create a vision of your future

Introduction

Romance takes center stage in most people's lives. More words are written and sung on this subject than on any other topic. It is one of the greatest sources of joy and excitement in our lives – and can also be the cause of heartache and pain. If romantic love is so pivotal in our lives, why do many of us struggle to obtain – and maintain – the relationship we desire? The problem is that most of us leave relationship success to chance. Whereas in other areas of our lives we learn skills and knowledge that will help us climb in a given field, we expect the world of passion and partnership to be something that comes naturally. This may be the result of early conditioning in which, once Prince Charming meets his princess, they live happily ever after. We like to believe that, in love, all comes easily, passion endures, and fulfillment is inevitable. The early days of courtship, with all the heady emotions and excitement, only serve to reinforce this delusion.

The belief that relationship success should come naturally and bring endless joy means that people are embarrassed about seeking help or buying a book for guidance, as they think the magic should happen automatically. It never occurs to them that guidance and skill are exactly what is needed to create the magic! This is where this book comes in. It takes a positive, theme-based, rather than rule-bound, approach to sustaining great relationships – hence the title, *The Mottos*. We all live our life by our favourite mottos, which we hear about from childhood. Mottos are phrases which encapsulate wisdom that we endeavour to live our lives by, and this book gives you the mottos to build and maintain a wonderful relationship.

This book begins with our top ten mottos. When followed, these will lead to lasting love. These are the key principles to ensure depth, stability and excitement in your relationship. While some of these may seem obvious, they need to be utilized together for maximum success. Overlooking one or two of these mottos can cause problems, as the mottos go right to the core of a relationship.

Part 2 deepens your knowledge base by giving you more specialist advice about enhancing your relationship. This section is packed with information and know-how to take your relationship to another level.

Part 3 addresses one of the most challenging areas of relationships – emotions and emotional management. So many relationships fail, not because of a lack of love and affection, but due to people's inability to effectively manage and channel their emotions.

Often relationships go into crisis over a specific issue. *Is he too young for me? Why is money coming between us?*

Part 4 provides insights into the root of these problems, plus practical advice to address these issues and prevent them ruining your relationship.

Part 5 takes as a starting point the truth that the work we do both on ourselves and collectively as a team in a relationship has a direct bearing on the quality of the relationship. So many relationships get 'stuck' because one party has not overcome particular problems, and this needs to be considered individually and in the context of the relationship. Self-fulfilment leads to relationship fulfilment – the more content you are with yourself, the more you are able to give to a relationship.

Part 1 – The key mottos

1. Understand what makes a relationship work

Understanding the mindset and behaviours behind a successful relationship is paramount. Many people dive into a relationship without understanding what will make their partnership go the distance. A successful relationship relies not just on passion and affection, but on understanding the key skills that make a relationship work. So what are these central principles? Each partner in the relationship should play an equal role.

There should be a balance in what the two parties contribute to the relationship in order to create a workable status quo. You do not have to contribute the *same* things; the key is to show that you are putting in as much as you would like to receive in terms of love, support and communication. Problems can arise in a relationship when one person perceives that they are giving more than they are receiving.

Both partners should feel some level of control. Clearly defining shared goals as a couple and working out the necessary steps towards achieving these will influence the direction you are heading in. There is also some psychology behind this. Creating joint goals allows us to feel a greater sense of control, so that we feel more secure in a relationship.

Positivity is important in long-term relationships. People like to be around positive people, not someone negative who will bring them down. A shared sense of humour has been shown to improve resilience in relationships, as well as communication: people are more relaxed when they laugh and are able to express their true feelings and release any pent-up emotions (such as anger) in a more positive way, which is more likely to lead to greater levels of trust and intimacy. By having a positive attitude to a relationship and being relaxed, you are more likely to make your partner feel happy and loved, as positivity is contagious. Being positive will also help you to cope more easily with any stresses in a relationship.

What makes us want to stay with someone for the long term can be very different to what makes us start a relationship. Real love is based on friendship combined with attraction – shared backgrounds, value systems and relationship goals, along with similar moral codes and mutual understanding.

People are extremely social creatures: we wish for someone we can communicate with and laugh with, someone who will support us.

2. Kindness is key

The golden rule of treating others as you would like to be treated by them allows us to reap rewards in our relationships. Furthermore, by being kind to others we are inadvertently also helping ourselves: improving our mood, strengthening our self-respect and confidence and making ourselves more attractive to others.

From an evolutionary perspective, the development and adoption of this rule makes sense. We are social animals, we live in groups, so reciprocity in caring behaviours, involving emotions such as empathy and compassion, to other members of our group is something that can only help our species to survive. Of course, to be motivated to effectively practice this behaviour requires us to have a healthy view of ourselves as equally deserving of receiving kindness from others.

Supporting this theoretical perspective is neuroscientific that suggests our ability to treat others with kindness is actually hardwired into our brains.

Dr Marco Iacobini[1] found that our brains contain 'mirror neurons' that automatically fire when we observe the actions of others, prompting us to naturally empathize with them – in other words, to feel what they are feeling. These neurons only stop firing when we attribute a negative label to the other person that dampens our empathic response.

Kindness can also be learned through a process of conditioning. When we are kind to others we are rewarded by the release of a cocktail of neurochemicals, such as oxytocin, serotonin and dopamine. These are known to improve our mental and physical well-being. This improvement in our mood makes it more likely that we will repeat that behaviour.

---

[1] Iacobini, M. (2009) 'Imitation, empathy and mirror neurons.' *Annual Reviews in Psychology*, **60**, 653–70.

So, why do we say that kindness can make us more attractive to others? Research has found that kindness and warmth are the most desirable traits in any type of relationship, and are considered even more essential than physical attractiveness when selecting a romantic partner. Professor Arthur Aron,[2] whose research interests including discovering determinants of successful long-term romantic relationships, states that being attractive 'doesn't help that much', suggesting that people tend to fall in love more readily with kind people, and arguing that kindness from both parties is the strongest indicator of a successful long-term relationship.

Decades of research by the Gottman Institute, an organisation that helps couples to build and maintain

---

[2] Aron, A. (2005) Why do we fall in love? (10 May). At: http://health.howstuffworks.com/relationships/love/why-do-we-fall-in-love.htm.

healthy relationships, goes some way to explaining why these traits are important. This may seem obvious, but they found that, in order for relationships to flourish, both parties' emotional needs have to be met, and that 'interaction styles' involving kindness and generosity (rather than contempt and disinterest) are preferred. Observing couples' interaction styles has enabled psychologists at the Institute to predict, with a 94% accuracy rate, whether or not couples will remain together.

There are a number of ways that we can become kinder:

- We can practise forgiveness and tolerance towards others – as well as to ourselves – for things that have happened to us.

- We can give our time to others less fortunate than ourselves, perhaps through volunteering.

- We can demonstrate random acts of kindness, either to people we know or to strangers.

- We can express gratitude to people who have shown us kindness.

Being kind to others does not mean that you should be taken for granted, and it is vital to recognise that there are some individuals for whom no amount of kindness will prompt them to similarly respond to you, respect you or even like you. Being kind doesn't mean that you have to be a doormat. You can be kind *and* assertive; they are not mutually exclusive traits.

The important point to remember is that, by being kind, you are respecting yourself and can be proud of your behaviour. Also, you are increasing your own attractiveness by being both kind and positive.

3.   Always be attentive

As time passes, we may allow other areas of our life to take center stage, and we may take our relationship for granted. However, being attentive to what is happening in our relationship, and the dynamic of the relationship itself, is crucial for ongoing success.

Here's what we need to pay attention to: *Reflect on your suitability*. We are attracted to people for all kinds of reasons. They may remind us of someone from our past. They may shower us with gifts and make us feel valued. Evaluate a potential partner as you would a friend: look at their character, personality, values, their generosity of spirit, the relationship between their words and actions, their relationships with others and how they treat other people.

Know your needs and speak up for them clearly. A good relationship is not a guessing game. Many people, men as well as women, are afraid to state their needs and, as a result, camouflage them. As a result, they are disappointed if they don't get what they want, and feel anger at their partner for not having met their (unstated) needs. Closeness cannot happen without honesty. Your partner is not a mind reader.

Respect, respect, respect. Mutual respect is essential for a good relationship.

View yourselves as a team. This means you are two unique individuals who bring different perspectives and strengths to your relationship. Remember, the value of a team is in combining your differences in a positive way.

Know how to manage your differences. This is a key aspect of success in a relationship. Disagreements don't sink relationships; name-calling and being uncommunicative do. Learn how to handle negative feelings and anger.

Stonewalling or avoiding conflicts is *not* managing them. Everyone fights at some point, even the best-suited couples. Arguments can be a healthy part of any relationship as long as you and your partner understand how to communicate and work out any issues in a calm, adult manner.

Communicate. If you don't understand or like something your partner is doing, talk about it and ask why they are doing it. Talk and discuss; don't assume.

Solve problems as they arise. Don't let resentments simmer. Most of what goes wrong in relationships can be traced back to hurt feelings, leading partners to erect defences against one another and to become strangers or, even worse, enemies.

Learn to negotiate. Modern relationships no longer rely on roles dictated by strict social norms. Because people's needs are fluid and change over time, and life's demands change too, good relationships are negotiated and renegotiated all the time.

Learn to negotiate. Modern relationships no longer rely on roles dictated by strict social norms. Because people's needs are fluid and change over time, and life's demands change too, good relationships are negotiated and renegotiated all the time.

Listen to your partner. Truly listen to your partner's concerns and complaints without judging. Much of the time, just having someone listen is all we need to solve problems; it opens the door to confiding worries and fears, which is at the root of real trust. Listening is not always easy. For example, imagine you have just come home from work after a difficult day. Your mind may be full of thoughts about work and solving problems, but if you continue to ponder these, you will find it difficult to truly listen to your partner, and they will realise this.

Instead, take the time to transition between work and home so that when you and your partner talk, you are focused on listening to them – not reviewing the day, generating ideas for tomorrow, etc.

Women tend to be good at multitasking. While this may be good in some situations, it is a barrier to truly listening to your partner.

Be empathetic. Empathy is crucial for a long-lasting, solid relationship. Remember to look at things from your partner's perspective as well as your own.

Work hard at maintaining closeness. Closeness doesn't happen by itself. In its absence, people drift apart and can be susceptible to affairs. A good relationship isn't an end goal; it's a lifelong process maintained through regular attention, communication, trust and respect.

Take a long-term view. A marriage is an agreement to spend your future together. Talk about your dreams regularly to make sure you're both on the same path. Update your dreams every so often.

Sex is good, but pillow talk is better. Sex is easy; intimacy is difficult. It requires honesty, openness, self-disclosure and vulnerability.

Never go to sleep angry. Say sorry to one another. Say 'I love you'. Be kind to one another.

Apologise. Anyone can make a mistake. Being able to say sorry is crucial (and highly predictive of marital happiness). Attempts to apologise can be clumsy or funny, even sarcastic – but being willing to make up after an argument is central to every happy marriage.

Practise forgiveness. The flip side of an apology is forgiveness. If your partner apologises, don't reject it. Accept it fully and put the fight behind you. Don't bring it up again in future disagreements.

Maintain some independence. Some dependency is good, but depending on a partner for all your needs is an invitation to unhappiness for both partners. It is unrealistic to expect one person to meet all your needs in life.

Maintain self-respect and self-esteem. It's easier for someone to like you and to be around you when you like yourself. Meaningful work – paid or volunteer – is one of the most meaningful ways to build your self-esteem and sense of self.

Keep things new. Enrich your relationship by bringing into it new interests from outside. The more passions in life that you have and share, the richer your relationship will be.

Cooperate. Share responsibilities. Relationships only work when they are a two-way street – with equal give and take.

Recognise that some times will be better than others. All relationships have their ups and downs. Working together through the hard times will make your relationship stronger.

Be self-aware. Make sense of a bad relationship by exploring what went wrong. Don't just run away from a bad relationship; you'll only repeat your mistakes with your next partner.

Use it as a mirror to look at yourself, to understand what you are doing to help create this kind of unhealthy relationship.

Realise that love isn't static. Love is not a static commodity that you're either in or out of. It's a feeling that ebbs and flows depending on how you treat each other. If you learn new ways to interact, feelings can come flowing back, often stronger than before.

4.   Set relationship goals

When it comes to relationships, many people expect fate to throw them in the path of their perfect partner. More people fail to make a relationship work because they think romance should 'just happen' than for any other reason. The fact is, people who are successful at maintaining an amazing relationship are proactive and positive about it. Somehow it doesn't seem 'sexy' to think about goal-setting in terms of relationships. We grow up reading fairy tales such as Cinderella, we watch romantic movies, and at no point does the romantic lead ever sit down and write a list of relationship goals – it doesn't fit the romantic image we dream of. The irony is, setting relationship goals is the best way to create your 'happy ever after'. In every other area of your life in which you want to achieve something you would set goals, make plans and take action, so why should romance be any different?

Be clear about what you want from your partner and relationship: Start by defining a few key needs you're not prepared to compromise on in your partner or relationship. It might be trust, kindness or a sense of fun, for example. Then think further about your key preferences in terms of the lifestyle you would like to have. This is not about creating a 'made to order' list of requirements, but about being clear about what you want – and what you *don't* want.

Set goals: what do you want to achieve?: Do you long to go out more with your partner? Have more fun together? Create more intimacy? Develop more common interests or a particular lifestyle? Improve communication within the relationship? Get married and have children? Be clear about not just the type of relationship you would like to have, but also your vision of the future and how you would like your relationship to be.

Plan for your goals using the SMART approach (specific, measurable, attainable, realistic, time-bound). Will you create date nights, factor in more time to talk, or make more time for intimacy? Whatever you decide, make sure your plans are SMART so that you can make yourself accountable and track progress.

Take action: Whatever you plan, make sure that you now take action. Make it happen. Taking action towards your goals will give you a magnetic energy which will draw the two of you together.

Take steps towards your goals every day and be positive in the face of any set-backs. Remember, the people whose relationships are the most successful are people who are proactive, aware and positive in their approach, whether this is to find a partner or to create a magical relationship. As the old adage goes, 'true love isn't found; it's built.'

Remember, we are conditioned to believe that we need to find one 'perfect' person who will meet all our needs for the rest of our life. The problem that many people have in terms of meeting suitable partners is that they confuse 'perfect for them' with 'perfect'. There is no such thing as a perfect person. None of us is, and expecting partners to be perfect will only result in disappointment. Stop expecting your partner to be perfect, or to fulfil your every need, and instead be open and willing to work on building the relationship that is perfect *for you*.

Make your goals specific: Setting specific goals in a relationship can help to ensure that you are on the same page as a couple – and it also helps to keep the relationship vibrant rather than static. There is also more chance that the relationship will succeed over the long term if a couple has shared values and their individual, relationship and long-term goals are complementary.

Goal-setting not only helps to outline what each person wants from the relationship; it also means you have the support of another person who understands you and what you are trying to achieve.

Outlining goals can help couples understand what's important to them both, and creates intimacy in the relationship as it encourages open and transparent communication.

The key point is to make sure these goals move beyond the general ('I want us to be happy') to the specific ('I want us to learn how to fight fairly and apologise to each other').

To ensure that you are a good fit with your chosen partner, here are some of the things to think about when approaching love in this way.

- What are your short-term goals?
- What are your long-term goals?

- Where do you see yourself in six months? A year? Ten years?

- Which areas of your life are you willing to make compromises in?

- Which aspects of yourself are you not willing to change? Why? (This will help you to enter a relationship with a better sense of your own identity and what you most value about yourself.)

- Do you want children?

Once you have defined realistic goals, then you can work as a couple to put steps in place to make the relationship work. If you have different visions, you may need to work together, communicate and look at ways that you can both compromise.

Make time to reassess your individual and relationship goals, as these can change over time, and you need to make sure that both people in the relationship feel that their needs are continuing to be met.

Though you must understand your partner's goals, you also have to take into account your needs. Taking a pragmatic approach to love and having more realistic expectations of relationships can actually be empowering.

This doesn't mean that chemistry, lust and attraction are not necessary; it's about making sure you have the best chance at love. When a person addresses their own needs, this tends to increase their self-esteem and confidence. Therefore, if you approach love in this way you are more likely to meet people who will be compatible with you, as well as increasing the chance of your relationship working out.

5.   Keep your expectations realistic

Everybody has ideas or expectations about their 'ideal' or 'perfect' partner and how they envisage their perfect relationship, and this is entirely natural. Our relationships form such a large part of our lives that it's natural for us to dream about what they should be like. However, when these ideas or rules become fixed or are unrealistic, we are automatically slamming the door in the face of our partner, and we're ignoring the fact that they are a learning, growing human being, like we are. When our rules or expectations are grounded in fantasy, rather than reality, they can be extremely damaging. Shedding unhealthy expectations is the first step to gaining a healthy, happy relationship. So what expectations can we keep hold of? Which are the healthy ones?

For example, we all want to desire – and be desired by – our partner. However, attraction is not based on physical appearance alone.

A huge number of factors play a part in how attractive someone is: their confidence, intelligence, the way they hold themselves, the way they move, speak, or even smell. Having a specific physical formula for a partner rarely works, and having tunnel vision means missing out on potential partners.

In other situations, it is not so much that one or two of our expectations are completely unrealistic; rather, we might have so many (relatively rational) expectations that we create a huge shopping list, not realising that there is no shop in the world that could possibly stock all those goods. Being too specific about what you expect leaves little room for anyone to fulfil your needs. However, it's important to realise which traits (such as respect and trust) are essential to you, and which are nice to have (such as being funny or dressing in a certain way). Expectations about the type of relationship you see yourself in can also be problematic.

Look out for contradictions in what you *think* you want, so you don't set yourself up to fail ('My perfect partner will be totally loving and attentive, yet still remain intriguing and mysterious'). It's critical to separate chemistry from compatibility, and check that you and your partner have enough of both – if you are enamoured with someone, it's easy to feel that nothing else matters. However, for a relationship to last, it has to involve more than lust. There should also be respect and friendship.

Don't expect the 'honeymoon period' to last forever. Chemistry does fade; scientists have managed to track this. They believe it's a hardwired 'love' response that evolved because it kept two people together long enough for their offspring to survive. They estimate that the honeymoon period lasts for about two years.

Expecting your partner to be perfect all the time is a recipe for disaster. Envision your 'perfect partner' as someone who is truly compatible with you, not someone who is literally perfect! Remember, your partner is human too: they will make mistakes, sometimes they will wish to spend time with their friends rather than you, sometimes you will argue. Having some conflict is normal; it's how we resolve difficulties that is important. Expecting perfection all the time will doom the relationship to failure before it has even begun.

Finding the 'right' man or woman will not fix your life or complete you, despite what you might see in the movies. However, the right partner will provide you with the love and support you need for a healthy and happy life. To achieve this, however, you need to accept that no couple is happy 100% of the time.

Being content in yourself is the key to having realistic expectations of your partner. When you are happy in yourself, you are in a better position to think about what your partner can expect from you.

The first step is to make sure you do not confuse unrealistic expectations with high expectations: this is a common mistake. High expectations do not need to be unrealistic as long as they reflect reality, following a true evaluation of yourself. Intelligent, successful and driven women are compatible with equally intelligent men.

The second step is to set boundaries and have a clear idea of what you will not put up with. Start with a little work on yourself: knowing yourself and being honest is a great first step to take. You should never compromise your core values in a relationship.

To identify your core values, start with the tangible elements. Work out what your views are on marriage, family life, male and female roles, etc. Look at your lifestyle, health and fitness habits (including smoking, drinking and/or using drugs), your energy levels, your interests, your life stage, your religious practices and political beliefs – even your location.

Also, ask yourself what kind of relationship would work for you. How do you respond to affection? What is your sex drive like?

Once you have all this information, stay open-minded. Many people can be compatible with you without sharing all your interests. So don't fall into the trap of thinking you have to have everything in common (except, of course, major long-term desires such as having children or not). Chemistry matters as well, but understanding the limitations of lust will give you a more realistic view of genuine love.

6.   **Build trust**

Trust and love go together. If you love, you trust your partner to love and care for you, no matter what. It is an expectation of behaviour.

Within a romantic relationship, as well in other types of relationship, trust grows gradually. Its formation is based on the consistency of expected behaviours associated with trust, such as what your partner says matching what they do. Is your partner there for you in a multitude of ways – emotionally, physically, mentally? By being there for someone, you allow your partner to rely on you and anticipate that you will be there for them in the future when they most need you. Only when there is a demonstration of steadiness in these behaviours and feelings do you feel a sense of trust building within the relationship.

At some point, you feel as though your partner has broken your trust. We are all human and make mistakes.

In a romantic relationship, if trust is broken on a small scale then you should focus on your partner's response. Do you both negotiate and repair the breach of trust, or does your partner respond defensively when you tell them you feel betrayed? Their response will show you what your trust means to them – and, in turn, what your relationship means to them. However, if trust is broken on a larger scale, such as infidelity, it can never be fully restored, only repaired. Again, it is down to what you expect from your partner and their response to the betrayal.

Sometimes, we carry mental scars from past experiences with us. It is imperative for a healthy relationship that these negative associations are left in the past, with your ex-partner, not brought into a new relationship.

For example, imagine someone who had a flirtatious ex-partner whose behaviour caused her distress. Eventually, the relationship ended. In a new relationship, it is natural to be more sensitive to behaviour that has hurt us in the past.

However, if this results in watching your partner closely in social situations, questioning him when he comes in from a night out without you, or avoiding introducing him to friends, then you are not giving your partner or the relationship a chance. New associations need to be made in relation to your current partner, as opposed to expecting them to keep to the same low standard as your ex. It is unfair to hold someone accountable for another person's actions. You need to wipe the slate clean and look at your new love with a new sense of trust. As Ernest Hemingway said: 'The best way to find out if you can trust somebody is to trust them.'

7.   **Put more in to get more out**

Business-savvy men and women tend to invest in their relationship using the same energy, creativity and passion that led to their career success. Seeking a partner should be viewed as an investment in your life, and should be approached using the same principles you apply to other major life decisions, such as finding the right job or the right home. In a partnership, we subconsciously rate ourselves on desirability factors such as physical attractiveness, intellect, social status, wealth, youthfulness and health. People with high levels of self-awareness and self-esteem are more likely to rate themselves accurately in terms of their compatibility with a partner. Once you have found a truly equal partnership (and remember, this is not solely a question of looks, which may not come into the equation at all, but equal in terms of outlook, values, hopes, dreams and beliefs), the next stage is to invest in the relationship.

Psychologists have recognised a parallel between economics and relationships: relationships work on an exchange of costs and benefits, similar to the marketplace.

A relationship will be successful if both partners perceive that the rewards, costs and contributions to the relationship are equal on both sides. As Eric Fromm, the German psychologist and philosopher, once said: 'Love is often nothing but a favourable exchange between two people who get the most of what they can expect, considering their value on the personality market.'

However, problems can occur when people take these kinds of business principles too far and expect to invest a minimum amount for a maximum return. Relationships, unfortunately, don't work like that – you can only get out as much as you put in (there is no such thing as a bargain!).

8.   Be aware of potential problem areas

Building a beautiful relationship also means being aware of danger signs. No one has a perfect relationship all the time. Couples often take each other for granted, give ultimatums, try to change each other and expect their partner to 'make them happy'. Part of building a strong, trusting relationship is being aware of potential problems and taking action early. Here are six common mistakes we make in relationships – and how to avoid making them:

1.   *Getting rid of excess baggage*

We all have a dating/relationship history. While it may be tempting to share our life story with our partner, certain subjects, such as the finer details of ex-boyfriends/girlfriends, should be left on the carousel at the baggage claim terminal.

Each new relationship offers the chance for a fresh start, but we spoil this opportunity when we reintroduce old injuries back into our life. If you have issues from previous relationships, you need to acknowledge, confront and overcome these before starting a new relationship.

2.   *The ex projection factor*

Just because an ex cheated on you doesn't mean that every other partner will too. It's a good idea to resist the temptation to project your ex's faults onto your current partner. Unjustified mistrust only creates further mistrust, damaging the relationship and making it difficult to develop intimacy. If you find you're revisiting past experiences and applying these in your relationships, it's time to stop – and give your partner the chance they deserve.

3.   *Being too picky*

Some people are too picky. There is a big difference between core values and preferences. Expecting honesty, integrity and a strong character are all worthwhile qualities, but 'must keep DVDs in alphabetical order' is not. Don't expect perfection in a partner.

4.   *Making a mountain out of a molehill*

It's very easy to make a mountain out of a molehill – sometimes we fail to see the bigger picture. Try to remember that people make mistakes. Your partner will, and so will you. Before you jump to conclusions, take a step back. It's rarely worth sweating the small stuff. For instance, if your partner is running a little late for dinner, it doesn't mean they deserve the cold shoulder or that they have done this to inconvenience you. Keep perspective on what's serious in the long term.

5. *Obsessing*

Try not to read too much into things that happen. Don't cling to each word, trying to work out what your partner is thinking; don't obsess about the look on their face when you use the word 'we'; and don't constantly look for signs that indicate how the relationship is going. Sometimes, if we behave differently because of what we *think* is going on, we can ruin a relationship that would have been fine if we'd just let things take a more natural course.

6. *Ignoring red flags*

If your partner is obviously not in tune with your most cherished values, pay attention to your instincts. If they become narcissistic (excessively selfish and uncaring of others), treat people rudely, hide their phone, or are increasingly critical of you, it's probably time to take action by challenging this behaviour, or move on before leaving becomes more difficult.

9. Maintain sexual and emotional intimacy

The concept of intimacy is often misunderstood in relationships. It is mistakenly thought to be simply physical, rather than a complex interplay of emotional, psychological and physical needs. True intimacy stems from physical and emotional closeness. Each impacts on the other, meaning that intimacy is either increasing or dissolving in a relationship. The need for intimacy often gets lost in a relationship, either due to the demands and drudgery of everyday life or because of misunderstandings between couples which are subsequently ignored or denied. Yet intimacy is what makes a relationship truly fulfilling, and makes people happy.

The impact of evolution

It could be argued that today, intimacy is more important than ever before in our close relationships. In the past, people lived in close proximity, in large families or communities: after all, we are social animals. Therefore many of our needs were provided for from this broader network from whom we could gain support and understanding. Today many people lead more solitary lives, and consequently need more from their significant other.

Sex and emotion are increasingly separated in society. The media focuses on sex, which suggest a dichotomy between physical and emotional needs. The need for true intimacy has its roots in evolution: it is human to long for a real connection with our families, friends, loved ones and partners.

The work we need to do on ourselves

Creating intimacy is not just about what we do in a relationship. Although it sounds clichéd, it is vital to know ourselves and our beliefs, and understand our desires and expectations before we can build intimacy with another person. We need to understand our attitude to relationships before we can build true intimacy with a partner. What we learned about relationships when we were young will influence our relationships today. Additionally, our beliefs will have led to experiences in previous relationships which determine how we interpret our partner's behaviour in our current relationship. Conflict in relationships is frequently caused by interpreting events in line with what happened in previous relationships rather than what is occurring currently. Understanding our biases and past hurts will help us to understand our responses. Furthermore, we have to be clear about our needs and expectations before we can communicate them to a partner – and being able to communicate them is the real key to intimacy.

The work we need to do with our partners

The biggest barriers to intimacy are misunderstanding and miscommunication. Most of us attempt to 'mind-read' our partners, filling in blanks, making assumptions and failing to see that what we perceive to be going on in their mind is largely based on what is going on in ours. To overcome this, we need to be open to listening to our partner and discussing our needs and expectations clearly with them. The most important thing to remember when listening to our partner is to understand that we are looking through different lenses. A deep understanding comes from empathy and perspective-taking rather than processing what we are being told through our own way of looking at the world. To do this well we must have an open mind. We must also avoid the tendency to engage in 'selective hearing' (when we only hear what is relevant or critical to us). The more you can change ways of relating that are not working, the better your chance of building the deep connection that can only come from a true understanding of another person.

It's the same for physical intimacy. You need to know your own needs and desires to be able to communicate them to your partner so that you can share a fulfilling physical relationship. A poor sex life is generally the result of poor communication and misunderstandings which are not explored, and so solutions never sought. Intimacy is a frequently misconceived concept in relationships, but its foundations lie in open, compassionate communication.

10.   Continue to cultivate new skills to create relationship bliss

'One of the most beautiful qualities of a relationship is to understand and be understood.'

Lucius Annaeus Seneca

There is a wealth of literature telling you how to make a great impression on those all-important early dates, but what about a few weeks and months down the line? This is when people forget about working on a relationship, and old behaviour which has tainted previous relationships may resurface. Many relationships break up, not because the people weren't right for each other, but because they are unaware of how to communicate and understand their partner. It's therefore worth honing your skills to create a special and meaningful long-term relationship.

Meet people on an emotional level first

This is an amazing skill which many people are unaware of. When one party is upset or unhappy, the other party often attempts to fix this by jumping into problem-solving mode or talking about their own experience. They are missing a vital skill.

To really connect with someone, you have to meet them on an emotional level before you share your story or try to improve the situation. Truly empathising with someone first makes them feel heard and validates their emotional response, which make subsequent problem-solving much easier.

Taking a moment to emotionally connect is one of the best skills you can use to bond in a long-term relationship. Do you know how to emotionally connect?

Develop listening skills

One of the first qualities to slip in a relationship is listening.

Feeling 'heard' is one of the key gifts a person can give their partner – and not feeling heard is one of the precursors to infidelity! Therefore remain attentive and attuned to your partner if you want to build an enduring relationship. Ensure you are really listening to what your partner has to say.

Show this by making eye contact, through your body language, and what you say when it's your turn to speak. Don't use the time when your partner is speaking to think about what you want to say.

Consider what your partner is saying as if you are standing in their shoes. Create a safe environment for you both to speak and show you are listening to each other.

Be able to laugh at yourself

Being able to laugh at yourself, and recognise (and apologise) when you get something wrong, is essential. Two of the most common complaints in long-term relationships are (1) partners who are 'high maintenance' and (2) partners who believe they are always right. Relationships should be fun, so we need to be able to laugh at ourselves.

Remember, you reveal your true self in a crisis

A tip for success in all areas of your life: remember that you show your true character when you're under pressure.

For example, one man was head over heels in love with his new partner until the night he stepped outside at a party and had a social cigarette with his friend. Unknown to him, his partner had strong views about smoking, and when she came across him having a cigarette she tore into him, reacting emotionally and erratically. He was taken completely by surprise and his view of her instantly changed. Had she waited until a suitable moment and raised the issue calmly, they may well have reached an understanding and he would have retained his respect for her.

So if you're having a difficult conversation or a disagreement occurs, guard against being defensive or over-reacting. Instead, try to understand the problem. Try to remain calm, genuine and focused in the face of conflict.

Treat your partner like a billion-pound customer

People frequently take their partners for granted, especially in a long-term relationship. This is partly human nature, but makes little sense when we consider that our partner is one of the most significant people in our life, and they therefore deserve the very best treatment. Everyone wants to feel appreciated. Appreciation brings out the best in people, which in turn feeds back into a successful relationship.

Relationships are the biggest source of joy in our lives, so it's worth learning how to nurture them. Remember that using even one new idea to improve your relationship will make a difference.

Part 2 – Mottos to help you prepare for your best relationship

Get an insight into your partner

Many people encounter difficulties in a relationship because they haven't found out enough about their partner. Often this is because we're caught up in the excitement of a new relationship, or equally it could be that we just don't wish to know, as we fear disillusionment or realising we are incompatible with the person concerned.

However, as all psychologists will say, past behaviour is the best predictor of future behaviour. This means that healthy, value-laden behaviours are repeated – but so are dysfunctional, negative behaviours.

It is therefore in our best interests to know something about our partner's past behaviour. Asking questions is not about judging another human being – we all have skeletons in our closet, and moments we are not proud of, and this is how we learn and grow. However, it is essential that we look out for ourselves and our future and make sure our partner is similar to us in terms of their values and the qualities they prize.

There are key areas which give insight into someone's character and value system. You don't have to probe or be intrusive or manipulative, but it is vital to find out certain information as early as possible, rather than months or years down the line, when it can be a shock. Getting insight into your partner happens through talking to them about a range of areas which help to reveal their personality. Unsurprisingly, most of these are to do with relationships. These are the areas to explore:

Relationship with family

The relationship a partner has with their family can reveal much. A key area to explore with men is the relationship they have with their mother – be wary if he treats his mother with contempt or disinterest, as a great deal of research supports the idea that 'as he treats his mother, so he will come to treat you'. Look out for respect, genuine warmth and compassion. The same can be said of women: how does she talk about her father? What is her relationship with her father like? How does your partner view their siblings or their children? Do they value these bonds and invest time in them? Be curious if your partner is reluctant to discuss their family. Of course, not everyone is fortunate enough to come from a happy family background, but someone with an unhappy childhood needs to have worked through any issues this has generated in order to be emotionally available for an adult relationship.

Friendships

Friendships give key insights into a person's set of values. Does your partner have long-standing friendships?

This indicates that they value longevity in relationships. Or do they have a more disposable attitude towards friendships, or see friends for what they can provide? If this is the case, you can predict what will happen to your relationship at the first sign of trouble! Does your partner value quality over quantity, or do they need lots of stimulation to massage their ego? Pay attention to how they talk about their friends.

Vision of the future

A key area to tap into is how your partner views the future unfolding. This is the key to aligning your relationship goals.

If having a family is central to your future, but your partner is undecided about having children, this is likely to cause heartache down the line. Where does your partner see themselves living in the long term? What sort of lifestyle are they hoping for? No matter how much chemistry is present at the beginning of a relationship, if one person loves spontaneity and the glitz of the city and the other loves routine and a quiet life, this will surface in the relationship with time.

Relationship history

This is obviously a key area, but it needs to be explored without being intrusive. Has your partner had previous long-term relationships? Is there a pattern in how their relationships have ended? How do they talk about their exes?

Be especially wary of people who are bitter about previous relationships or those who take no responsibility for the end of the relationship. It goes without saying that if someone is derogatory about their ex-partners, this should ring a warning bell – most people have been hurt in a relationship, but are able to discuss this without criticising their exes.

How they feel about their career

A person's career reveals a lot about their traits and

characteristics. How does your partner feel about their career? If they are a manager, do they respect and care for their staff? If they have a boss, are they disparaging about them? (If so, be wary.) Has your partner taken responsibility for their career, moving on when the time is right or displaying loyalty if the position is valued? How do they talk about their colleagues?

Do they ensure that work is balanced, with time for other essential areas of their life? This is also an area where you can assess how ambitious someone is and how that might be a positive or negative contribution to the relationship. Career often aligns with attitude towards lifestyle as well, so if someone has a passion for their work, and continually seeks to develop themselves in their work, they often have a passion for living and a curiosity about life.

When exploring these topics, don't interrogate or judge your partner – this will put someone on the defensive and may lead to secrecy or withholding of information. Allow people to tell their story, and try not to be judgemental if you don't like what you hear – everyone wants to be accepted for who they are. However, you also need to know who your partner is, so be alert to what is not right for you so you don't waste time in the wrong relationship.

Put time and thought into your relationship

Relationships can be exciting and heady, but they can also include vulnerable stages in which we are either carried away or hitting problems, and this is when we are most likely to overlook logic or be swept away by emotion, lust and dreams about the future. Here's what you need to consider:

1. Don't confuse lust with love. During the initial stages of a relationship, many of us are guilty of doing this. Don't rush into any

commitments too quickly, as further down the line you may find that those feelings you were experiencing were lust, nothing more. Love is based on more than attraction and chemistry.

2. What are your partner's values? When you get into a relationship, ensure you take the time to establish what is most meaningful to your partner. More importantly, what do they expect from a relationship? Many relationships end due to differences in values and relationship goals.

3. Turn a positive into a negative. When forming a romantic relationship, think about your past relationships and why they did not work out. Was there anything you could have done differently that may have saved the relationship? If so, and if it is relevant to

your new relationship, make sure to apply these changes, to give you and your new partner the best chance of success.

4. Let your partner know they are on your mind. For many people, the road to success is not an easy one, often requiring high levels of dedication and long hours in the office. If you leave for work before your partner, send them a text at around the time their alarm goes off. This will make your partner feel loved and remind them that, although you are not with them, they are never far from your mind.

5. Remind them that you care. As you 'grow in' to a relationship it's normal to feel comfortable, but it can be easy to take your partner for granted. Unfortunately, this is never good for relationships. In order to

give your relationship the best chance of success, make sure you regularly remind your partner how much you care for them. This can be done in a variety of ways, such as a compliment, holding their hand or bringing them a cup of their favourite tea before you leave for work. Little gestures like these are how we cement a relationship.

6. Accept your partner for who they are. You cannot enter a relationship with someone and expect them to change to fit your lifestyle. If you are from very different backgrounds, whether this is a different culture, religion or class, learn about your partner's background. Additionally, learn to accept not only what you love about your partner, but those habits you may not be so fond of. Remember, there are probably

things you do that they don't like. Don't highlight their shortcomings – this will only lead to negative feelings towards you and insecurity on their part, both of which can damage a relationship.

7. Remember, a relationship is a two-way street. Show respect to your partner and treat them in the way that you wish to be treated. Having mutual respect will encourage you to think about your partner's feelings and to acknowledge them as being as serious as your own, even if you do not always agree with the way they feel. For example, if your partner is angry with their sibling but you think their sibling has a point, try to see things from your partner's perspective and empathise with them rather than challenging them.

8. Make time for each other. Maintaining a family and a career can be difficult but, irrespective of how busy your life may be, ensure you make time for your partner. While you may not have time to go on a date every week, try to set aside an hour before bed when you can talk to one another and share your thoughts, feelings and any worries. Be supportive of your partner if they are going through a tough time at work or facing other difficulties. Remember, even if you cannot provide practical help, emotional support is just as necessary. This could be as simple as a hug and reassuring them that everything will be OK.

9. Tell them how you feel. It is important to show your partner how much you care, but sometimes it is better to tell them. We all

appreciate a romantic gesture, but don't forget to talk to each other as well. The moment you stop communicating with your partner is when you begin to distance yourself from them.

10. Maintain a sense of self-respect and identity. While we all long to be the best partner we can be, this does not mean condoning or tolerating any form of abuse directed at you (or your children). Any abuse – whether it is physical or emotional – is a clear sign that you should end the relationship and seek professional support.

What women really want.

It is true what men say: women are complicated! Many women may think, 'I want to be swept off my feet by a handsome, successful, powerful man.' However, some socially confident, successful women feel that men are too often intimidated by their success.

They believe men feel insecure if they are not the higher earner or the more well-known partner in the relationship. These women may dominate at work (sometimes in traditionally male careers) but they do not want to dominate when it comes to men and relationships.

But why is this? Throughout the animal kingdom, females do not mate with males until the male has made some kind of aggressive display.

Scientists say this display shows us that the male is strong, can fend off competition and will therefore be a good provider and protective to a female and any young.

This may be where our need for a strong alpha male comes from. Although this is still key today for survival among animals, it is much less true in relation to today's emancipated women. However, we must remember that our genes take a lot longer to change than our social environment.

So, while male animals perform aggressive displays to impress a potential mate, humans prefer something more acceptable and subtle: dating. In the Western world, tradition says that men should take the initiative, put themselves out there, risk rejection and make the first move in approaching women.

This is just one example of acceptable aggressive behaviour women want from men (initially, anyway). While this is a good starting point, it is not enough. In a longer-term relationship, many women wish men would take control in other areas.

This explains why many women, irrespective of how successful they are, want a man who is more successful than they are, at least as wealthy as they are, and as fit and healthy as they are. So many successful women look for an alpha male, even if their logical mind is screaming, 'I do not need a man who will play hunter-gatherer and fight other men for scarce resources so my children and I can survive!'

Let's face it, today women can provide everything they need for themselves, yet our genes haven't realised that yet. So if you think that you crave one thing in a man, but are constantly drawn towards something else entirely, perhaps the above might help explain why.

Does this mean women are all gold-diggers? Absolutely not! Most of the women are not motivated by money alone. They are interested in the personality traits of successful men.

Once upon a time, food was the scarce resource that we wanted our men to fight for, and the most dominant men had the healthiest children. Nowadays the same personality traits can allow a man to accumulate today's scare resource: money! Having said that women can provide everything we need for ourselves, we should point out the obvious: we do tend to look for someone to father our children. We look for certain traits in men that lead us to believe they are both fertile and likely to want to settle down, and also that their (our) children are likely be successful genetically. Indeed, the basics of physical attraction are formed from this premise. Women have also become body language experts. Our senses tell us if a man is interested in what we are saying, if he is listening to us, if he is genuinely concerned for our well-being, and so on. We use these skills to judge how much a man likes us, and we want a man to show he has a connection to us on this emotional level before we begin a sexual relationship.

For women, attraction in long-term relationships is much less based around the evolutionary factors above. What makes us want to stay with someone is very different to what makes us enter into a relationship and fall in love. Longer-term attraction is predominantly based around social factors: shared backgrounds, shared value systems and similar moral codes, mutual understanding and shared relationship goals are all essential.

Women are extremely social creatures. We want a partner we can communicate with, someone who can stimulate our mind. We want a dedicated partner who is faithful. We want to be supported and respected. Sex and chemistry always remain influential, and we want a partner that we feel a physical, as well as an emotional, attraction to.

Happiness goals – are you and your partner reading from the same book?

'Happiness is when what you think, what you say, and what you do are in harmony.' Mahatma Gandhi

The Art of Happiness, by the Dalai Lama and Howard C. Cutler,[3] is the sort of book you can dip into for solace and, more importantly, direction. It never fails to inspire with its words of wisdom. In this book, Howard Cutler asks the Dalai Lama how we can best connect with others. The Dalai Lama suggests that developing empathy – seeing things through the eyes of others – is an essential part of the process.

Further questioned by Cutler, the Dalai Lama says that empathy could also be developed by approaching

---

[3] Dalai Lama & Cutler, H.C. (1999) *The Art of Happiness* (Hodder & Stoughton).

relationships with the understanding that, despite the differences between us, we all are united by a common goal: to achieve happiness rather than suffering. This unity allows us to respond to each other on the same level, even if we don't agree with another's definition of happiness and/or the methods they are using to achieve it.

While we can develop empathy and respect for other people's goals, what happens when we find ourselves unable to match our partner's focus and plans for achieving their own happiness goals? Is this important?

Actually, it is. Little research has been carried out into the specific goal of happiness in romantic relationships. However, we can look at a recent review of the literature surrounding factors associated in long-lasting marriages.

This research suggests that sharing common life goals is one of the significant factors involved in relationships that are both long-lasting and rewarding.[4]

How do you find out whether your partner has similar goals to yours? One way is to talk to them, early in the relationship, and ask them about their life goals. What do they wish to achieve? What makes them happy? Then ask yourself how much you empathise with, and share, their views and goals. At the same time, you would expect your partner to ask you the same questions and show an interest in your life goals. This increases your confidence that, while you might not always be on exactly the same page as your partner, or even in the same chapter, at least you are reading the same book!

---

[4] Parker, R. (2002) Why marriages last: A discussion of the literature. Australian Institute of Family Studies, Research Paper No. 28. At: www.aifs.gov.au/institute/pubs/RP28.html

How to keep your relationship alive

When you first met your lover, you probably couldn't get enough of each other. You spent all your free time together and, when you were apart, you probably thought about one another all the time. This is known as the honeymoon period. When you progress past this stage to a more mature love, you experience comfort, deeper intimacy, security and stability. Here you are settled, secure and loved, and for a while you are content. However, you may begin to look back and miss those intense, romantic and passionate early days.

Your partner's presence set off a chain of chemical reactions inside you, most notably the rapid production of the hormone oxytocin, which is known as the love hormone. The production of oxytocin is a natural response to a pleasurable experience, such as being around your lover.

Oxytocin therefore acts as a reinforcer, encouraging us to spend more time doing what feels good (in this case, being with our lover), which is essential in the early stages to form a bond. This enables us to create a strong foundation to support our relationship through the latter stages. Many people feel disappointed when this intense period wears off. However, all is not lost. You can still have passion in your relationship!

How to keep passion alive

There are many ways in which you can ensure that the passionate side of your relationship continues and your love deepens:

Quality time: Set aside quality time to spend with your partner – for example, arrange a date night – when neither of you has any distractions competing for your attention. This will give you the opportunity to truly be in the moment with your partner and allow you to learn new things about them.

Value and appreciation: Spend time alone, and think about what you appreciate your partner for. Show your partner that you value them and appreciate them. Tell them what they bring to your life. You can do this verbally and non-verbally – remember, actions often speak louder than words. Your partner will probably reciprocate, making you both more excited to be around one another.

Spontaneity: Being spontaneous and surprising your partner with gifts, notes or gestures of love can bring novelty and excitement back into your relationship. Try leaving your partner a love note on the fridge or a sexy voicemail letting them know you're thinking of them.

Engage in new activities, together and alone: Studies show that doing new things together increases passionate love and, subsequently, satisfaction within a relationship. Be creative! You don't have to do new things together. If you enjoy a new activity you do alone, this will increase your sense of well-being and will be reflected into the relationship, creating a deeper sense of passionate love. *Make exciting plans for the future*: For example, plan a dream holiday or short break just for the two of you. Even if the circumstances aren't right to actually get away at the moment, simply looking through holiday brochures, talking about what you would love to do and what excites you will inspire you both.

Psychologists agree that it is vital to retain a sense of self in a relationship, and to develop that sense of self to allow the relationship to continue to grow and thrive.

Improve emotional communication with your partner
Do you speak the language of love? We all know that communication, both verbal and non-verbal, is crucial in relationships. It is essential that both partners in a romantic relationship understand the meanings inherent

in the messages and behaviours expressed by the other. In short, they must speak the same language.

But when it sometimes seems as if you and your partner are from different planets, how can you achieve this? The answer may lie in Dr Gary Chapman's acclaimed book, *The Five Love Languages*.[5]

Chapman suggests that every individual has a 'primary love language' and, in order to feel truly loved and valued in a relationship, this love must be expressed to the individual in their preferred 'love language'. Verbal or non-verbal, the key to success in all interpersonal relationships is the *expression* and *receipt* of love. It is crucial that people communicate their love in ways their partner will understand.

---

[5] Chapman, G. (1995) *The Five Love Languages: How to Express Heartfelt Commitment to your Mate* (Northfield).

Chapman distinguishes five love languages, and notes that each language has a certain way of expressing and receiving love, which should be tailored specifically to the needs and desires of the individual.

To ensure long-lasting love, not only should you learn to speak your partner's love language, but you must be fully fluent.

The five love languages are:

Words of affirmation: Individuals for whom this is their primary love language experience love through receiving emotional support, praise or encouragement. Being told 'I love you', hearing the reasons why they are loved, and receiving unsolicited compliments are prized above all non-verbal gestures of love. It is noteworthy that, for these people, verbal insults and hurtful remarks can be devastating and are not easily forgotten.

Acts of service: These individuals feel loved when their partner does practical things that help them. In other words, actions speak louder than words for these people, and they appreciate practical help and support. For example, it may mean more to them that their partner runs them a hot bath and allows them to have a couple of hours to themselves after a particularly tough day than trying to talk to them about it.

Receiving gifts: Putting an effort into carefully selecting a gift make these individuals feel cherished. Gifts are interpreted as showing that their partner is thinking of them, cares for them and understands their likes and needs. Consequently, a missed birthday present or inappropriate card would be an issue for these people.

Quality time: Individuals whose primary language is 'quality time' experience love when they receive time and undivided attention. They feel loved when they have a sense of togetherness with their partner. It doesn't matter what they do, as long as they are focused on one another. This can be an important way of showing love if time is precious. For example, one couple who both had busy work projects demonstrated their commitment to the relationship by always clearing time from midday on Sunday to go for lunch and a walk.

Physical touch: This is the language of individuals who experience love through their partner's physical presence and contact. These individuals interpret appropriate physical touch and proximity to their partner as signs of care, support and affection. Neglect or physical abuse is therefore highly destructive to people for whom this is their love language.

According to the love languages above, different people 'speak' different love languages and, as is the case with the spoken word, it is easier to communicate in your native language. You can adapt your natural tendencies to ensure you express love in ways your partner understands and prefers, and this may be seen as a greater expression of love, thanks to the effort you have made. Your partner should also try to communicate with you in *your* love language – the best relationships are based on communication and equal respect.

It is necessary to note that within the five distinct love languages there are innumerable ways of expressing love, so you can be as creative as you like and are limited only by your imagination! Furthermore, as with all forms of language acquisition, the more you use your partner's love language, the more comfortable and proficient you will become in this secondary language.

For example, if your partner's love language is quality time, you need to make a conscious effort to give this to them, and they also need to try to express love in your language.

When both partners alter their behaviour to fall in line with the other's, they will feel more loved, happy and secure. The simplicity of this reasoning does not undermine its potential power.

As stated above, when in a loving relationship, it is imperative that both partners show and are shown love. Therefore, when the main difficulty in a relationship is the surface-level communication of love, these simple behavioural changes could lead to massive improvements in the relationship.

This novel conceptualisation of emotional communication within relationships therefore has significant implications for those who wish to make their relationships more mutually fulfilling and rewarding.

The book may also be helpful for people going through difficult periods in their relationships, and it may also provide valuable insights for people who are single and would like to develop more meaningful future relationships.

The concept does not focus on understanding and exploring the emotions that underlie people's need for love to be expressed in particular ways; it does not address deeper emotional problems within a relationship. Consequently, it does not teach people how to love and connect with their partner on a more fundamental level. The ideas in the book are not a 'fix-all' for all relationship problems, but are a positive, practical way of enhancing an already loving relationship.

Using and applying love languages can greatly enhance even the best relationships by ensuring that both partners know that they are loved, so reading this book may help you to improve your relationships.

The primary source of miscommunication in relationships

'He just doesn't listen… He doesn't even try to understand me, let alone talk to me. I can't talk to him any more.'

'She says I don't listen. I try to be supportive but it's never enough. I constantly feel rejected, like I'm not good enough.'

Do either of these sound familiar? We all want a fulfilling relationship. This is achievable – but sometimes we expect it to just happen. However, we need to put in a little work first. At some point, most couples will find themselves in conflict. Don't worry, as this is natural. Early on in a relationship, conflict can occur for a variety of reasons, mainly because each person is exploring whether they are compatible by expressing their values, goals and beliefs to the other. They are getting to know each other.

Conflict in relationships can escalate from something very simple, often a misunderstanding of the other's perspective. It is essential to remember that everyone is unique, and no two people will ever think the same about everything. Also, bear in mind that men and women differ quite drastically in how they interpret certain situations. Therefore we sometimes have to try to understand the other's perspective rather than assuming everyone thinks as we do.

It is said that men are from Mars and women are from Venus, so a clash in communication is bound to occur. Perhaps by understanding where the miscommunication arises, we can spot it and prevent problems from escalating. So let's look at two examples of the most common forms of miscommunication that arise in relationships.

Men in their caves: Ladies, if your partner is quiet, feeling down and does not respond to your support, then it is best to leave him alone and give him some space. According to relationship expert Dr John Gray, author of *Men are from Mars, Women are from Venus*,[6] when stressed, men often retreat into what he describes as a 'cave' – their own quiet sanctuary where they can relax, wind down and recharge. What is important to know here is that wanting to spend time alone does not mean he is neglecting you or does not want to be with you. Men and women have different ways of dealing with emotions and stresses. Women usually like to talk about their problems and be heard, while men may prefer to pull away until they have managed to find a solution to their worries. Don't mistake this for neglect or disinterest. Don't resent him or take it personally, since fighting with your partner

---

[6] Gray, J. (1992) *Men are from Mars, Women are from Venus.* HarperCollins.

or trying to force him to open up will make him more likely to retreat further into his cave.

One example of this was when a man was suddenly made redundant. He became quiet and reflective. His partner felt shut out, and began to question him about their relationship, which only added to his stress. Had she understood that this was his way of processing and solving the problem, rather than taking it as a reflection of how he felt about her, a lot of arguments could have been prevented.

The blame game: Gentleman, here is something you should know by now: women like to talk! When stressed, women will express their frustration by talking, probably to the person they feel most comfortable with and closest to – you. Take this as a compliment and keep this in mind.

Next, remember that they are venting their anger and

frustration *towards* you, not *at* you – there is a big difference. As previously mentioned, men like to solve problems. They don't usually talk just for the sake of it – they have a goal in mind: to fix the issue. Women don't always share this goal; talking is enough to make them to feel better. Therefore, if you try to 'fix' her problem, you accidentally overlook her emotions and focus on the end goal, making her feel like you are not listening to her, which in turn makes you feel blamed for her anger. Women often just want to be heard and reassured. All you need to do is listen and respond to her emotions, not her words.

Understand the differences between how men and women communicate

Many a relationship fails because of misunderstandings that occur due to the different ways in which men and women communicate.

Complaints such as 'he didn't understand me' and 'she was impossible to deal with' are often cited as reasons for relationships ending, yet are often entirely avoidable. People focus on the content of conversations without really understanding the differences in communication between men and women – which can lead to problems. The tragedy is, if people don't understand communication styles and their own role in the breakdown of communication, they take these problems into their next relationship and create exactly the same circumstances. This is why people may split up with numerous partners for the same reason.

Understanding differences in how people communicate will help you avoid pitfalls and will instead foster closeness and understanding. This will help us to avoid George Bernard Shaw's caution that, 'the single biggest problem in communication is the illusion that it has taken place'.

Men and women approach communication differently

Men and women often have different goals and needs in communication. If we are unaware of this we can be hurt, offended or even exasperated when our partner's response is not in accordance with our expectations. For example, studies indicate that communication styles differ in a crisis. Men often tend to problem-solve (offer a solution in an attempt to solve the problem as quickly as possible), whereas women tend to empathise and seek mutual understanding. If these underlying motivations are not understood, men may feel frustrated about the time it is taking to discuss a problem, whereas women could think that a man is being dismissive. Recognising different communication styles and understanding where they come from means we can adapt our responses to avoid problems. This is worthy of consideration, as we tend to underestimate how much relationships can be enhanced by talking.

You are and your partner are not the same person

This is the starting point for great communication, yet this seemingly obvious observation is actually the least remembered in relationships. We get frustrated when we expect our partners to view the world, process information and communicate in exactly the same way as we do. On an intellectual level we would argue that we understand how background, experience and physiological differences combine to make each person view and interact with the world in their own way. However, on an experiential level we often default to thinking our partner is just like us and should be expected to think and communicate in the same way as we do. This is especially true if the conversation is emotive! So keep in mind that if your partner is responding to you in a way you find challenging, this does not make them wrong. Attempting to look at things from their perspective and 'walk in their shoes' is an instant defuser and gives you an insight into how to communicate and connect with them.

The single most common complaint women and men have about how their partner communicates

Women often complain that men interrupt them, and that they have to talk faster to get their point across before they're interrupted. On the other hand, many men get frustrated when women speak elaborately and at length, but take a long time to make their point. So perhaps there is a case here for women to be concise and clear in order to have their points understood, and for men to be wary of interrupting. On a related note, any man out there who finds it hard to decipher a woman's needs, take comfort from the words of Freud, who once stated: 'THE GREAT QUESTION THAT HAS NEVER BEEN ANSWERED, AND WHICH I HAVE NOT YET BEEN ABLE TO ANSWER, DESPITE MY THIRTY YEARS OF

RESEARCH INTO THE FEMININE SOUL, IS "WHAT DOES A WOMAN WANT?""

Mind-reading and hint-dropping

Men often complain that women expect them to be mind-readers rather than saying straight out what they need. This sets up a cycle of women hoping men will understand what they mean without having to tell them about it, and women subsequently becoming resentful that their partner hasn't intuited what they need. This same problem occurs with hints – men generally find it difficult to pick up hints, and if they do catch on they may well feel resentful that their partner has not addressed the point with them directly. Both parties should ensure they raise issues promptly and clearly.

For example, one woman felt that her relationship with her partner would be enhanced if they created more space in the relationship and if she restarted some of her old hobbies. Instead of bringing this up directly, she suggested that her partner should meet up with old friends and take up cricket again, which confused him as he didn't understand the reason behind her comments. Avoid miscommunication and confusion by raising topics in a direct manner.

On affection and emotion...

There are differences in the way men and women express affection in friendships and relationships. Men often tease and are sometimes sarcastic with their friends, whereas women are more direct at communicating affection, and tactile in expressing it. A budding relationship may never start if the woman interprets teasing as dislike rather than admiration. Additionally, men frequently find it hard to understand emotions that are not explicitly verbalised, while women pick up quite easily on emotional cues. Understanding these differences can go a long way to understanding our partners and preventing misinterpretation.

During conversations with your partner, be mindful that men have a different perspective, a different physiology and a different communication style. An awareness of these differences is central to communicating well.

Make time for love

Sometimes, maintaining a successful career and a relationship, along with various other commitments, can seem impossible. We all know the danger of not putting enough effort into our romantic relationships. Yet we still find it very difficult to do 'more', however much we may long for more attention, appreciation and intimacy ourselves. How do we make time for love?

Plan a date night: While you may not have much spare time, make sure you schedule some quality time with your partner, doing something special to you both.

This will give you something to look forward to. During stressful times, having something to look forward to evokes feelings of excitement and joy, which can lift us when we are feeling down.

Use technology: If your work requires you to travel, you may be away from your partner for long periods of time, which can put a strain on the relationship.

To ease the fact that you are away from them, arrange a time to speak over WhatsApp, Skype or webcam. Speaking to your partner face to face (well, almost…), despite the distance between you, keeps communication going and means you stay involved in each other's lives.

Make sure they know you are thinking about them: Although your partner may understand your busy lifestyle, it is crucial not to take this for granted. You don't want your partner to feel neglected!

To stop this from happening, send them little reminders that you are thinking about them. This can be as simple as sending them a text message in the morning just to say hello and that you miss them. Reminding your partner that you miss them as much as they miss you will make them feel more secure in the relationship and remind them of how important they are to you.

Resolve arguments: Time away from your partner can be an opportunity to resolve conflict. In the heat of the moment an argument can escalate and we end up saying things we regret. Having some time away allows you to step back from the situation, reflect on any issues you are having, and address them when you are feeling calmer and more level-headed. By the same token, do not use this as an excuse to avoid confronting a situation or even as a way to punish your partner by not speaking to them, as this could make the problem worse.

Let your partner know you love them, but you're upset with them at the moment and need some time alone to calm down.

Snatch the small moments: It's easy to fill time with trivialities. These are the moments that you and your partner could snatch to build real closeness. Having a quick glass of wine together before bed, or taking a moment to light some candles before watching a movie, can add romance and ambience to your evening.

When you are travelling, think about how you could treat your partner or make them feel special.

Schedule trips away: However busy you are, blocking out time in your calendar, just as you would do for other areas of your life, is the key to creating magic. Getting away is a treat for the brain as it is a complete break from the norm and all your senses have new experiences to process. Who better to share this with, and create new memories with, than your partner?

It is not easy, but you *can* have a successful career and a successful relationship. Taking on board these simple ideas can help your relationship blossom, even during your busiest times.

Understand the science of love

Attraction is an significant part of a relationship, but what defines attraction is more than just physical appearance. Factors such as a sense of fun, compassion and communication can also play an important part in maintaining a relationship. Another vital element is similarity. We tend to be more invested in a relationship when we have joint interests, so emphasise the parts of your relationship where similarity exists, such as background, intellectual curiosity, values and lifestyle. For a relationship to last, a couple must have a similar outlook on life, and both may need to make compromises by adjusting their life goals. This can explain why shared experiences are so important in helping to keep the attraction alive in a long-term relationship.

Why do we find ourselves attracted to some people, but not others? What is the chemistry that people talk about as being an essential part of any romantic relationship – and is chemistry really far-reaching? To begin to answer the first question, we need to take a quick dip into the complicated world of neuroscience. Neuroscientific research uses brain imaging techniques to identify the complex systems of chemical messengers, neurotransmitters and hormones that are activated in certain parts of the brain when we see an object we desire.

When we are attracted to someone, hormones are activated in our brain. They have an influence over the more rational, decision-making parts of our brain. This helps to explain why it is sometimes difficult to think clearly when we are very attracted to someone. There is indeed *real* chemistry involved in attraction.

When people fall in love they may experience physical symptoms, such as impulsive feelings, finding it hard to concentrate, losing their appetite or their focus at work, or finding their priorities have changed. They may have less interest in friends and family, or spend time daydreaming, desperately waiting for their phone to ring.

When we fall in love, brain imaging has shown that our frontal cortex tends to shut down. This is the part of the brain that is vital for judgement, which is why we might act a little out of character. To add to this, the anterior cingulated cortex is activated, which is associated with feelings of euphoria. This cocktail of chemicals is the 'natural high' we are all seeking.

However, this state does not last for ever. We know that passionate love tends to fade over time. Couples often worry that they don't feel the same as they did when they first met, and that something might have changed. This is not bad news; *au contraire*! After the honeymoon phase of a relationship, which usually lasts for a maximum of two years, our brain's reaction to the chemicals mentioned above decreases, allowing us to enter a calmer, longer-lasting phase of our relationship.

The importance of being honest about your feelings

Honesty is one of the most paramount aspects of a healthy, loving relationship. Honesty is the foundation of trust and intimacy, which leads to the happy, successful relationships we all aspire to have. It creates less worry in a relationship, which in turn creates a better you. The more you trust your significant other, the easier life seems. This is because honesty is exceptionally important in all aspects of a couple's life, from discussing how to parent, to deliberating about finances to everything else in between, as it allows you to feel open and understood.

Concealment of the truth causes far greater pain than the truth itself, as it demonstrates a total disregard for your partner's feelings. This is because, when you enter a relationship, you begin to share your life with someone. A huge part of sharing your life is being able to understand them and their perfectly imperfect quirks.

When one partner is dishonest, it jeopardises the understanding you have of your partner, and vice versa, which can bring numerous aspects of your relationship into question. Once trust is broken it can never fully be restored, so it is imperative that you are always honest with your partner. It is easy to forget that in a relationship you are continually learning about your partner, and that dating your partner should continue throughout your relationship.

It is also good to be self-aware. If you are not being honest with your spouse about your feelings, the chances are you are not being honest with yourself.

By burying your head in the sand, you are putting your mental health at risk. You may feel anxious or unsatisfied with how things are panning out for your relationship.

Your partner will also try to fill in the gaps that your lack of honesty creates. Consequently, they may believe you are thinking and feeling something completely different to what you are, which may cause problems.

It is far worse to conceal your true feelings than it is to tell your partner the truth. It is vital that you feel you can be honest in your relationship. Also, you must remember that you and your partner will feel differently about certain situations, and that is OK. It is how you communicate, and deal with, your differences that will determine the success of your relationship. Simply going along with your partner's feelings to keep the peace will lead to resentment.

Being honest with yourself and your partner about your feelings is incredibly important. It leads to a healthier mind, a happier partner, and an open and loving relationship.

How to be mindful

Being mindful and living in the moment is the road to happiness in relationships – and life. To illustrate this point, imagine this:

You are dancing, feeling self-conscious, aware of your body and of other people watching you. You feel stiff and fidgety and you can't enjoy yourself, but you feel you have to carry on dancing.

Now imagine a second scenario. You are dancing: you feel as free as a bird, there is a huge smile on your face, you feel the music and you move without thinking. You are not consciously aware of your body or other people watching you; you are just having a good time.

In the first scenario, you are not being mindful. In the second one, you are.

Buddhist monks began to practise mindfulness more than 2,500 years ago. Mindfulness is essentially a state of heightened awareness of, and attention to, the present moment, while taking a non-judgemental and non-evaluative approach to one's experience. This is also significant for successful dating.

Mindfulness has been positively correlated with higher marital satisfaction, empathic concern, effective communication and adaptive response skills when faced with relationship stress. As well as relationship satisfaction, mindfulness approaches have also been associated with increased sexual satisfaction. Women who practise mindfulness often say it allows them to be more aware and present during sex.

So often, we have so much on our mind that we forget to be mindful and live in the present; we allow time to rush past, unobserved and unseized.

We squander the precious seconds of our lives as we worry about the future and dwell on the past. When we are not in a relationship, we fantasise about meeting our perfect partner; when we meet someone, we fear that we are missing out. We give in to intrusive memories of the past, or fret about what may or may not happen in the future.

In comparison, mindful people focus on the present. They tend to have higher self-esteem, are more accepting of their own weaknesses, fight less with their romantic partners, are more accommodating and less defensive. As a result, mindful couples have more satisfying relationships. People who are mindful focus on enjoying the moment they are in and making it the best it can be.

To become more mindful, start with day-to-day things like making a cup of coffee. Very often when we are talking to our partners our brains are multitasking, thinking about the next day or a problem at work.

Instead, concentrate on one thing at a time so that you are able to focus on what your partner is saying. When you are out with your partner, be present. Instead of planning the future or talking about a problem, take the time to focus on looking at each other, appreciating your time together and behaving as you did on your early dates, when you felt like there was no one else in the room.

You will find that your relationship deepens and you maintain the spark that drew you to each other in the first place.

The power of forgiveness

What is the meaning of forgiveness? Forgiveness is often referred to in religious and spiritual contexts, but it also has a power in romantic relationships.

To forgive means to stop feeling anger or resentment towards someone or something. It is a conscious decision that we make in order to inhibit those particular feelings. Resentment comprises three basic emotions – disgust, sadness and surprise – and is essentially the perception of injustice. We can forgive those we feel have let us down, whether it is deserved or not, but this requires us to be willing to let go of feelings that have caused us great pain. Consequently, it is important that we identify the source of our feelings before we forgive, otherwise we are not dealing with the basis of our resentment. Forgiveness is often thought of as regaining a neutral state within a relationship, but it is often difficult to forgive a partner. It may feel as though we are giving up or allowing our partner to get away with the behaviour you feel has warranted the contempt: however, this is certainly not the case. It is advisable to forgive: not only will it create balance in your relationship, but it will allow you to be compassionate with yourself. If unresolved, bitterness can chip away at you and affect your outlook on future relationships, making you defensive or untrusting. The first step of forgiving is having a clear understanding of what has happened, how you feel about it, and communicating this to your partner. It will allow you to take responsibility for your feelings. You are both involved in what has caused resentment in your relationship. That does not mean you are at fault, but that essentially we must all take responsibility for how we feel and how we can prevent feeling contempt towards our partner.

The ability to forgive has been linked to overall relationship satisfaction. The reasoning behind this is due to a decrease in conflict. Forgiveness is cathartic and therefore has remarkable health benefits, both psychologically and physiologically. Forgiveness also leads to less stress and fewer symptoms of depression.

Forgiving does not necessarily mean forgetting, but it gives you the chance to grow and learn – about both yourself and your relationship.

Essentially the power of forgiveness is its ability to let you be the best version of yourself, so you can find the power that forgiveness brings.

Part 3 – Mottos to help you handle emotions skilfully

How to overcome jealousy

'Plain women are always jealous of their husbands. Beautiful women never are. They are always so occupied with being jealous of other women's husbands.'
Oscar Wilde

As mentioned earlier, evolutionary psychology has shown us that men and women value different characteristics in a partner.

Men value physical attractiveness in women because it is related to her fertility, whereas women value dominance in men as this is related to a man's ability to provide resources. Like many emotional adaptations, jealousy is a flawed and often exaggerated call to arms. That is because the human life span was, until not long ago, much shorter. Evolutionary psychologists and anthropologists believe that our ancestors rarely got a second chance to woo a mate. Our ancestors succeeded in acquiring a mate long enough to procreate – those who couldn't are ancestors to no one. It makes sense, then, that humans developed jealousy as a built-in infidelity detection system, in this competitive social cauldron.

What causes jealousy?

- Low self-esteem – a person with low self-esteem may feel so undeserving of being loved that they can't believe that their spouse could possibly remain faithful to them.

- Feelings of insecurity – these may stem from low self-esteem, or may be related to instances in which we have previously been hurt.

- A fear of vulnerability – this is the inability to let our guard down and let another person know us completely.

- Distrust.

- Uncertainty and loneliness.

How do you stop jealousy?

1. Try not to take part in self-defeating behaviour. If you are questioning or making accusations, stop immediately. Whether you need to literally bite your tongue, go to another room, or talk to a friend, don't allow yourself to continue this destructive behaviour. Usually people engage in self-defeating behaviour because initially it reassures them and makes them feel better. But remind yourself that feeling better is

just temporary and it is a destructive behaviour that must stop.

2. Challenge your irrational thinking. Identify how your thinking is irrational, and remind yourself of this whenever you have jealous thoughts. It is often beneficial to write down irrational thoughts. On closer inspection, it may be obvious you have no reason to be jealous (perhaps because of all the loving things your spouse does for you).

3. Work on improving your self-esteem. Remember that jealousy is not about others, but about you. Use your jealous feelings to remind yourself that you need to focus on improving your self-esteem. Give yourself positive self-statements and do things that make you feel good about yourself.

4. Learn to be vulnerable and to develop emotional intimacy. For any relationship to be successful, you must be able to take risks. There are many ways to do this. For instance, if you feel insecure, you might share these feelings with your partner and talk about ways they can help you feel more secure. Or, if you are afraid of being vulnerable, try to share your worry with your partner.

Sometimes the process of developing awareness and challenging irrational beliefs can be too difficult to accomplish alone, and you may need assistance from a therapist. A good cognitive behavioural therapist will be able to help you with these types of worry and doubt. They can help you identify where you are going wrong.

Are you engaging in so much negative self-talk that you need help to change this destructive behaviour? Do you have unresolved issues from a previous relationship? Do you lack self-confidence and have a low perception of yourself? Jealousy can destroy a relationship and can stem from a wide combination of all of the above. However, with help, you can get back on the road of positivity and make current or future relationships work. You will also be better able to establish what went wrong. This will give you the self-awareness to halt any destructive behaviour in the future.

Let anger guide you, rather than control you

Some anger is healthy. Anger has an evolutionary purpose: it allows us to fight back when necessary and to stand up for ourselves in life. We have probably all found ourselves in situations where we feel angry and have found that this anger is actually doing us much more harm than good. There are times we don't want to be angry, or it doesn't serve us to be angry – when we can get a better result by being considerate and calm. It is only possible to achieve this by taking responsibility for our anger.

Once you are aware that your anger is your responsibility, the key is to catch initial anger-inducing thoughts and replace them by calm thoughts.

For example, if your partner plans to go out with their friends rather than staying in and having dinner at home with you, instead of immediately assuming the worst ('She *knew* I wanted a quiet night in!', or 'I *knew* he didn't want to spend any quality time with me!'), take a more considered stance. Give your partner the benefit of the doubt. Think of alternative reasons why your partner may have chosen to go out, such as 'Perhaps he didn't realise I was hoping to have a quiet night in tonight', or 'She did say she was hoping to see her friends this week'.

Remember, healthy long-term relationships are based on trust and respect.

By becoming aware of which thoughts trigger anger, you can choose to control your emotions. It really is that simple. However, we sometimes need to express our anger, so how do we this healthily?

'Venting' is a term used to describe the expression of intense emotion, often with the purpose of getting rid of frustration.[7] The purpose of venting frustration is to feel free of it.

However, before we vent our frustrations in a relationship, we must assess *why* we feel the way we do.

Self-awareness: The first step on your journey to uncover truth involves self-awareness. Often frustration is a side-effect of deeper issues. In an attempt to resolve this, we may find that we subconsciously project our

---

[7] At: www.thefreedictionary.com/venting

feelings on to our partner. We may feel insecure, jealous, paranoid or anxious, but whichever undesirable emotion is preoccupying our thoughts and influencing our behaviour, we must learn to first recognise it and then separate it from our relationship with our partner (unless of course it is caused by their actions).

For example, imagine a man finds himself becoming irritable with his partner over trivial matters like burning dinner or forgetting to pick up the dry cleaning.

To both, this initially looked like a problem with the relationship, but by becoming self-aware the man realised that pressure he was experiencing due to his mother and aunt being ill resulted in him becoming less tolerant towards his partner. This was the issue that needed addressing, as it was the root of the problem.

Seek guidance: It may be helpful to seek guidance from a non-biased, trusted friend or family member. This will enable you to determine whether your level of frustration is rational or slightly delusional, as this unhealthy emotion can taint your perception. If you do this, you will have discussed the situation at least once before you decide to confront your partner. This will help you to focus your thoughts more logically and, hopefully, harness your emotions so you handle the situation calmly. If you feel the need to cry, get angry or act in any other way to feel better, do it.

You may also find it therapeutic to exercise, pamper yourself or write down your thoughts.

Venting as an opportunity: Using venting as an opportunity is critical, not only to understand yourself better but also to understand your self-worth, because you deserve the best. Although frustration is unhealthy, having emotions is not. It's what makes us human. n your mind. Discussing your feelings openly and honestly with your partner can relieve stress.

One woman who had been brought up to always keep the peace and never complain found it very difficult when problems arose in her relationship, because she felt she had to keep smiling and soldier on.

This resulted in pent-up emotion, which was finally released in an explosion of emotion and behaviour which proved detrimental to the relationship.

As she learned to express frustration and deal with issues as they arose, her emotional health, sense of well-being and her relationship all improved. We all need emotional validation from time to time, so remember that what you are feeling is completely fine and is a basic human need.[8]

Ultimately, venting frustration in a relationship should be done with integrity and respect. Act according to your values, try to understand the situation from the

---

[8] At: www.psychologytoday.com/blog/the-squeaky-wheel/201106/the-antidote-anger-and-frustration

other person's perspective, and remember that your approach should always be expressed with the goal of a positive outcome. Releasing emotions in anger threatens your relationship. Once you have acted, you cannot take back your outburst, so ensure you are true to yourself and fair to your partner.

Stop insecure thoughts and behaviour

Which single personality trait makes you most popular, attractive and sexy? It's nothing to do with being tall, slim, beautiful, wealthy or ultra-intelligent; rather, it's everything to do with being confident. People are attracted to people with high self-esteem. If a woman or man genuinely believes in themselves (which should not be confused with arrogance), people are instinctively drawn to them.

Unfortunately, far too many people, rather than feeling confident, feel insecure. Insecurity stems from a wide variety of reasons. It can be as a result of overexposure to the culture of comparison encouraged by social media and today's consumer society. It can be the result of a hurtful comment made years earlier, such as being called fat or ugly or stupid. Sometimes people are driven to succeed to mask their insecurities – but no matter how successful you become, you will always demand more from yourself as the insecurity driving you still remains.

The good news is that insecurities do not have to remain with you. To start with, you need to manage the source of your insecurity.

- Learn to think and speak differently. Don't pepper your talk with put-downs; find another way to converse. Remember, it's not your job to automatically fill any gaps in a conversation or provide amusement. When you fall into self-critical thoughts, note them. Once you are aware of them, make a deliberate effort to change them to positive thoughts: for example, by thinking about something you like about yourself.

- Avoid people who sap your self-esteem, either by putting you down or by building themselves up so much that you feel inferior. Instead, mix with people who, because they believe in themselves, are secure enough to let you do the same.

- You may feel that you need to hide your successes – that you feel undeserving and unworthy. But it's vital to acknowledge them to yourself – and to let others realise you're doing well. So be proud of your victories, and share them with others. Celebrate and reinforce the message that you're worth it.

Know and develop yourself

- Try not to judge yourself for the things you can't control or lack; instead, focus on what's going on internally. Try to reset your expectations. Set yourself new challenges. For example, if you feel shy, join a reading group or some other type of activity that will let you ease into social interaction. You can't develop if you never push your limits.

Look and act confident

- It's an old adage, but feeling good about yourself on the inside will make you feel great on the outside. Small changes can give you an extra boost to your self-esteem.

- Use positive body language to appear more confident. Stand tall, be happy and approachable, be confident to take up space in your environment, keep an open and approachable posture, and work on identifying habits you display when you are nervous, like fidgeting. Most of us have one or two unconscious 'tells' that give us away, but once we are aware of them we can make an effort to fix them.

- Ask for support – having family and friends to share our struggles and successes with makes our journey much easier and less intimidating. Accepting help from those who care about us will also strengthen our resilience and ability to manage stress.

- Anticipate obstacles – we will inevitably face them. This can help us stay on track.

- Don't beat yourself up – perfection is unattainable. Remember that minor missteps when reaching our goals are completely normal. We should resolve to recover from our mistakes and get back on track.

Attractiveness is about more than just having a pretty face, but we usually think our physical appearance is most important when deciding whether or not we are attractive. Women tend to keep a close eye on their weight, and they spend on average £36,000 on hair care over their lifetime. Men think about their stature, physique and hairline. We all have a tendency to focus on our appearance without realising that the most significant factor in attractiveness is something entirely different: self-confidence.

When someone is confident, they transform the energy in a room. We are drawn to them: we want to be their friend, to talk to them – and to date them. In the world of dating, confidence is essential. Someone who doubts their own appearance and ability sends signals of insecurity that warn off potential partners. If you are dreary and dull, people will want to avoid you. If you are bright and vibrant, people will want to be around you.

There is, however, a thin line between confidence and arrogance. Overconfidence is a negative trait and a turn-off for most people. The quietly confident, self-assured person who is not afraid to show their vulnerability usually wins over the brash self-assurance of the overconfident.

Keep your emotions in balance

Psychology has been successful in highlighting the nuances of human connection and how people behave.

Our assessment of our own mental health is most closely connected to our sense of success in the emotional and the professional spheres. To paraphrase Freud, if we are achieving our potential, engaging socially and professionally, and at the same time have good and meaningful emotional connections with other people, we feel good, our mental health is good, and we are happy. If mental health depends on love, what does love depend on? The answer is simple – on our readiness to form emotional bonds. An emotional bond is a requirement for a good relationship. It indicates that some individuals are significant to us, that they matter, that we have a sense of belonging, and that we treat these individuals in a special way. The need for affectionate bonding is deeply rooted. Our first experiences of bonding with important figures (our parents) in many ways determine our patterns of connection and bonding in relationships for the rest of our lives.

Everyone desires to connect with other people but many do not succeed, due to various fears.

First, there is the fear of intimacy. People who are afraid of intimacy have superficial relationships, often based on sex, and they do not allow themselves to open up and share.

These behaviour patterns are often related to a fear of rejection: they think they will be rejected by their partner once they discover what kind of person they really are. At the core of such a fear is low self-esteem and, consequently, a deep sense of unhappiness.

Thus, individuals with low self-esteem are likely to be unable to connect with their partner in any meaningful way. They may have experienced rejection and suffering in previous relationships. Since they avoid intimacy, they feel lonely and empty and they compensate for their feelings of insecurity with constant flirting and short-lived sexual encounters.

These give an immediate short-term confirmation of their own value ('people don't want to have long-term relationships with me'), which further hinders their ability to connect.

Second, there are individuals for whom partnerships – relationships based on love – are the only purpose of living, and who feel that they do not exist outside this kind of intense relationship. They are able to create connections with significant others quickly and easily, and commit to every relationship. However, they often have difficulty in setting boundaries between themselves and their partners, who they see as their only source of security and happiness. This type of bonding is fine at the start of a relationship. Soon after, however, the partner begins to feel under pressure. Emotionally dependent individuals tend not to show responsibility, but insecurity and low self-esteem.

Having a healthy connection to another person is based on trust, and their readiness to be part of a relationship, and at the same time being aware of your own and your partner's needs.

Healthy connections are coupled with healthy boundaries. Connecting to another person means allowing that person to get close to you, to reach your inner being, and allowing yourself to show intimacy and tenderness. Bonding is a prerequisite for true love and good relationships.

When they are assessing their partners, many people rely on 'chemistry' or 'intuition', which are basically unconscious processes that may be based on childish or unrealistic fantasies. While chemistry is crucial and intuition can play a part, true love includes a realistic and accurate assessment of a partner. It is important to know yourself: to know what you desire from a partner and a relationship, the needs you expect to be met by your partner, and what your values are. Values are things we believe in. This could be a religion, the importance of family, or having children, or spending time together; it could also mean the importance of your career, or characteristics such as honesty and intelligence. 'Values' may also mean intrinsic core values – for example, one person may value loyalty and commitment to a relationship, whereas another might value freedom and the option to practise polygamy!

When we recognise our feelings, we have control over them. We start loving someone once we have ascertained that they meet our criteria and we are sure that they are becoming meaningful and valuable to us. However, the criteria we set must be realistic and attainable.

Every relationship undergoes certain phases – attraction, collecting information (partner's personal history, their values, attitudes, goals), assessment (to enter the relationship), and emotional bonding (being ready to get closer to the other person and establish a relationship).

Three factors are crucial for establishing a genuine emotional connection:

- a balance between giving and receiving
- compatibility
- sincerity.

If we are living without a love that is based on these values, then we are living in a world that has no emotional value.

Understanding an unemotional partner

Everybody has emotions. However, how well people express their emotions varies from person to person. If someone is *emotionally available*, this means they are able to share their feelings with another person. An unemotional person is out of touch with their emotions and is unable to define or express them in a healthy way.

Why are people sometimes unemotional?

The ways we express emotions are learned in childhood. An unemotional person may not have been taught how to express their emotions as a child, or emotional expression may have been discouraged. In addition, for men, the expression of emotions may be perceived to be unmanly. For example, a boy may be taught that 'big boys don't cry', so they may see showing emotion as a sign of weakness. In addition, they may feel scared and insecure about expressing their emotions if they have been hurt in the past. An unemotional person may be afraid of losing control if they express their emotions. Emotions can be unpredictable, and an unemotional person may feel safer intellectualising their experiences through logic rather than allowing themselves to simply feel.

They may find it more comfortable to internalise or rationalise their emotions to themselves than to express them.

How does emotional unavailability affect a relationship?

An emotionally available person who is with an emotionally unavailable partner can be affected in the following ways:

- They may feel insecure in the relationship and unsupported by their unemotional partner.

- They may feel rejected or unloved when their partner avoids speaking about their feelings, or avoids conflict.

- There may be a breakdown in communication, as the emotionally available person may feel as if they are not 'allowed' to express their emotions either.

This can lead to many unresolved issues within the relationship.

- Emotional connection is an important aspect of a relationship. When this is not there, the emotionally available person may feel distant, detached or cut off from their partner, and also unheard, as their partner may be unresponsive when it comes to talking about emotions.

- Continually feeling rejected can affect the emotionally available person, and can lead to feelings of not being good enough, isolation and loneliness.

- A lack of emotional expression may also mean that there is a lack of intimacy in the relationship. For example, the unemotional partner may not initiate physical gestures of affection such as hugs or kisses. Instead, they may express their feelings in other ways, such as buying their partner presents instead of saying 'I love you'.

- There may be a lack of empathy in the relationship as the unemotional person struggles to understand the feelings of their partner. This can lead to the emotional person feeling misunderstood.

- The unemotional person may express their emotions in an unhealthy way. For example, they may bottle up unexpressed feelings until they erupt in anger, or avoid talking about their feelings by burying their head in the sand. They may hope that doing this will avoid any conflict. However, this often only makes things worse.

- The unemotional person may also have developed unhealthy ways of dealing with their emotions, such as using drugs or alcohol to help them to numb their feelings, which will further negatively impact on their relationship.

What can you do if you have an unemotional partner?

- Healthy relationships consist of balance, as one person cannot meet all our needs. It is essential to keep a range of interests outside the relationship. This can provide an important social network for the emotionally available partner, and it also removes unhealthy pressure from the relationship.

- Find an activity you enjoy doing together and bring the fun back into your relationship: this is a first step towards building intimacy. Spending regular quality time together can help strengthen your emotional connection. Communication is another influential aspect of a relationship, and open communication will help to build trust.

- Communication does not always have to be verbal. Non-verbal communication, such as body language and eye contact, is a powerful way of encouraging an unemotional person to express their emotions. They may find it easier to show their emotions than talk about them. Learning more about your partner's non-verbal communication can help you to understand more clearly what they are trying to say to you.

- Break patterns of negative behaviour and try something new. If you can identify the problems within your relationship, it will give you the power to make good choices and to break these patterns of behaviour. As a couple, you can begin to identify each other's needs within the relationship. It is not just about learning about yourself, but also learning about your partner and how to support them. Look at what is missing from your relationship, whether this is passion, commitment or intimacy, and discuss practical ways to make positive changes.

- Another important tool is modelling your emotions. In other words, if you long for your partner to express their emotions in a healthy way, then you need to express yourself in this way first. One way could be to use 'I' statements when expressing your emotions, such as, 'I feel that…'. If you express your emotions in this way, your partner is less likely to feel attacked, is more likely to understand your point of view, and may be more open to talking about their emotions in the same way.

- Focus on your present emotions and feelings – avoid bringing up past conflicts or arguments. If you focus on the here and now, you are more likely to understand each other and move towards finding a solution. For example, one woman who found it difficult to open up found herself feeling even more remote when, during arguments (which were due to her being unemotional), her partner kept bringing up recriminations from previous rows. This led to a vicious cycle where she found it even more difficult to express emotion. She was not devoid of emotion; she simply found it difficult to express her emotions. As her partner found new ways of communicating with her, which were not argumentative or accusatory, she began to trust him more, and new communication – both verbal and non-verbal – opened up between them.

- Take the time to listen. When we have strong emotions, we may feel hurt and want our point of view to be heard. This can mean we become defensive and may not hear our partner's point of view. In this case, both people in a relationship may feel misunderstood. Try and listen to what your partner is saying without interrupting them or becoming defensive. You are more likely to understand your partner in this way, and they are more likely to understand you. Remember, it takes two people to make a relationship work.

- At times it may be easier to work on emotional expression in a neutral environment. You may wish to seek professional help and to see a couples therapist together if you are both willing to work on your relationship. Individual therapy may also give you a space to heal from emotional issues.

Don't give in to emotional blackmail

Many children discover that crying, even if it is not genuine or heartfelt, will elicit the response they are looking for, such as getting to stay up later, or the toy they want in a shop. This is normal and, as they grow, most children learn that there are better ways of asking for things they want.

Some adults, however, still practise this type of toxic emotional blackmail. It comes in many forms, from using emotion to control others through making them feel guilty, to threatening a loved one with withdrawal of your love if they do not give you what you want.

Emotional blackmail is a powerful form of manipulation. Typically, emotional blackmailers will know their victims well and will be aware of all their weaknesses and vulnerabilities.

They may want something they know their victim is unlikely to comply with, and may use threats, or make them feel guilty. A typical example of this type of emotional bullying is to say 'If you loved me, you'd do this for me' or 'If we can't agree on this, perhaps we should split up'. Another example is a man who has previously prioritised work to the detriment of his relationship – his partner continually reminding him of this means that he feels guilty and is more likely to do whatever his partner asks, whether he wants to or not.

The usual response to emotional blackmail is to resist, then to give in – because of how much the victim values the relationship and because the blackmailer has usually pressed all the right buttons and worn them down. Unfortunately, emotional blackmail keeps going.

When you give in to a blackmailer's emotional threats, an unpleasant cycle will develop which can be very difficult to stop.

As a victim you can lose all sense of boundaries and end up agreeing to things that you do not want.

This can slowly destroy a person, as they lose their sense of self and become immersed in a toxic relationship in which they have little control. They are very vulnerable. People who use emotional blackmail are generally narcissistic, with little ability to self-reflect and little understanding of personal responsibility.

If you find your partner uses emotional blackmail as a normal part of your relationship, talk to them about it and suggest couples counselling. If they do not agree to work on this issue, or continue to use emotional bullying tactics, it is best to leave them and seek support from your family and friends or professionals.

Someone who is narcissistic is unlikely to change, or be able to provide what you need to ensure a healthy loving relationship.

You can't change someone else; you can only change yourself and your own behaviour – and how you react to someone else's behaviour.

Overcome negative emotions about past relationships

Many of us look back at past relationships with sadness, regret and sometimes bitterness. We have a tendency to think that if a relationship has ended, it has 'failed'. However, many relationships are meant to run their course, and even if there were problems that led to a break-up, we can all learn from past relationships. Although there can be negative reasons for couples to split up, it is productive to look at past relationships through a positive lens – both parties were probably doing their best, given the person they were at the time. This can be a difficult concept to accept, but holding on to bitterness or resentment about previous relationships will affect your current relationship.

Focus instead on how your past relationships can provide insights you can use to help create your ideal partnership now.

In order to learn from past relationships, you need to think about how both parties behaved. Always take responsibility for your own actions and remember that it takes two people to create conflict in a relationship: both people have choices about their behaviour and whether or not they stay in the relationship.

It is also important to identify any patterns that keep occurring in your relationships. Consider why this is happening. Is there something you need to address in yourself? For example, someone with poor self-esteem is likely to set their sights lower rather than higher when it comes to what they will accept in a relationship, often settling for someone who treats them badly, as this is all they think they deserve.

If this sounds familiar, you must identify the root cause of the issue in order to have a healthy relationship.

Whatever has happened in previous relationships, don't take these issues into the future. Nobody wants to pay for the mistakes of a previous partner, so it is important that you don't anticipate your current partner will behave the same way as your ex did. This can be very difficult, especially when trust has been given and broken, but it is essential to give every relationship a chance, and have faith in your increasing wisdom and ability to identify and resolve any problems that arise.

We can learn a lot about ourselves from past relationships. With the right mindset, there is no such thing as failure. So you may not have had a great relationship in the past, but you have probably learned something valuable from it that will help you in your current partnership.

A positive person will take the time to assess, as fairly as possible, what went wrong and how they can prevent the same thing happening again. But how can you be fair when you're angry and upset about something that happened? Try to remember that a good partnership is about compatibility between two people; it's not about who's right and who's wrong.

Don't get emotional; get smart and logical

We've all had arguments with our partners over silly things. Precious minutes, hours and even days can be wasted feeling upset and angry over a fight or overthinking the things you said: 'I wish I'd said that differently!' 'Why did I say that?' 'I didn't really mean it!'

So, what can we do in order to avoid arguments like this?

- *Are you hungry/sleep deprived*? If so, it's normal to be irritable and distracted. Consider whether your feelings are being exacerbated by your biological needs. Walk away from the problem for now and come back to it when you are feeling more yourself.

- *Is it the right time?* Sometimes we don't really think things through; we jump to conclusions. We may later realise that the issue wasn't that important or that we could have handled things differently. It's sometimes best to cool off and reflect on what caused the initial argument, and give your partner time to do the same too. Being a couple also means respecting each other's space and meeting each other halfway.

- *Don't make it personal.* The most long-lasting damage that arises from an argument is when a fight becomes personal. Try to stick to the problem in the most objective way possible. Insulting your partner with contempt or sarcasm, or making fun of their looks, intelligence, job, or family, is not behaviour that belongs in a loving relationship. Avoid making general comments such as 'You always...' or 'You never...' – they are unhelpful, and will only result in a defensive reaction and consequent mutual criticism. Stick to the matter at hand and be specific: say, for example, 'I was upset when you were late home and didn't ring me to let me know, not 'You're always late! You never ring me to say where you are!'

- *Communicate.* Letting the other person explain themselves, maintaining eye contact, being understanding and showing mutual respect (not interrupting or walking out of the room) are effective ways of disentangling a problem and fully understanding each other.

Remember that you are not there to judge whether what your partner is saying is true or false. All their feelings are valid, even if you do not agree with them. For example, if your partner feels that you been neglecting them, listen to why they feel this way. In turn, try to explain how you feel. Keep the conversation open and communicative. Don't walk away or sulk. Try to be objective and don't resent your partner for communicating their feelings to you.

All couples argue sometimes. In fact, arguments dealt with in a healthy adult way can lead to a stronger relationship. When all you want to do is stamp your feet and shout, remember that having a healthy communication style will help you and your partner to solve any problems more quickly and will lead to a better relationship for you both.

How not to be emotionally distant

Sometimes the safest thing we feel we can do in a relationship is withdraw (and this can sometimes be true, but not if it's a maladaptive way of dealing with pain in a relationship). Withdrawing can feel empowering at the time, but it can cause devastation to both parties in a relationship, and is a very unhealthy avoidance strategy. Additionally, it can become a template for future relationships.

The 'self-disconnector' has usually had negative emotional experiences that have made them feel unlovable and unworthy. They believe what their ex-partner(s) said about their flaws. Result? They detach from their 'worth' and try to find worth in their partners instead.

What sort of life experiences can make us behave this way?
We develop attachments and relationship patterns very early in our lives. Psychologists believe that these patterns are developed between birth and seven years old – the imprint period. We learn them unconsciously from the relationships we have with our primary caregivers. It is thought that what we learn at the unconscious level at this age will stay with us and affect our behaviour and choices throughout our lives (unless we become aware of these patterns and act to change any negative ones).

Being rejected by someone who features heavily in your life as a child, or having an absent parent, is a common reason for an individual feeling that they are not worth people's time and attention, or that they are unlovable.

Some individuals will be more self-aware. They may be able to reflect and unlearn this kind of unhelpful thought. But if someone believes they are unlovable, this will play out in their relationships. This can usually be seen in the type of people they are unconsciously attracted to – someone they believe is too good for them, who they place on a pedestal. They may not set healthy boundaries, and tend to become co-dependent, believing that without their partner they are worth nothing. Having this type of mindset also means that they are more likely to believe any criticism and negative feedback they are given.

What are the best ways to stop this behaviour?

The more we know about ourselves, the more choices we have. We can *choose* not to behave in a certain way. First, we have to be willing to see the part we play in attracting certain relationship issues into our lives. If you struggle with this, ask a couple of your closest friends to write a paragraph describing you. Others may see your self-destructive behaviour patterns more easily than you can.

A good way to choose your next partner is to focus on finding people who share your values, beliefs and goals.

If you are in a relationship that is not working, and you still think it can be improved, reset your boundaries by first deciding what you will and won't accept in a relationship, then making these boundaries clear to your partner and adhering to them.

Perhaps you have always put your partner first and put yourself second – for example, by having sex when you're really too tired. Be clear about your own needs – in this case, your need for rest rather than sex when you're exhausted. Resetting your boundaries may come as a shock to a partner who has always had things their way in a relationship, but you will need to be firm. Your partner should want you to feel more confident and secure.

Resist the temptation to 'rescue' your partner

There are some people who repeatedly find themselves in relationships with people who are needy, emotionally damaged or going through a particularly difficult time. These people are known as *rescuers*, and they usually feel the need to help others so that they feel valuable and approved of themselves. They stay in relationships with people who have problems, as this makes them feel valued and wanted. However, this is obviously not a healthy reason to be in a relationship. Rescuers attempt to fix, or save, their partner. They do this based on the – usually misguided – belief or hope that, with their help, their partner can be fixed and can become the person they really want them to be. Unfortunately, this rarely happens. In reality, giving your all to fix, change or save your partner, especially when your efforts and energy are not reciprocated, will ultimately leave you drained, resentful and unfulfilled. Eventually you will feel that you have no other option but to leave. You may then promise yourself that you will not repeat this in future relationships. You may resolve to find a partner who will support you too, rather than the other way round. However, time and time again you find yourself trying to save your partner.

Why do we choose partners we feel we have to save?
Why do so many of us make the same mistakes again and again when it comes to people we date? We see our friends in loving relationships with partners who look after and support them, but we can never seem to find this for ourselves. Very often the problem stems from childhood. If they way you experienced love as a child was to 'do as you were told', and if you were obedient you then got love and approval, you are likely to repeat this pattern now. This is because you experienced love as *conditional*. On the contrary, if you felt loved as a child despite getting into trouble and getting things wrong, you are likely to have grown up with a good sense of self-esteem and confidence, and are now probably less reliant on approval from others.

How can we change this pattern of behaviour?

The best way to break this pattern of behaviour is to sit down and look at all the significant relationships in your life. Spend some time reflecting on what they have taught you, and thinking about what you want – and need – from a future relationship. This will help you start to think more clearly about the type of relationship that will work best for you.

In order to have a successful relationship, you first ned to have a healthy relationship with yourself. If you have an internal need that hasn't been fulfilled, such as the need to be accepted for who you are, you will probably try to obtain this from your relationship.

For example, if you were criticised a lot as a child you may feel that you are never good enough, so you look for approval in a relationship, which leads to rescuing behaviour (so that you feel you are useful and valuable to someone). If that relationship does not work (and the chances are it will not), you will seek approval again in next relationship. This is how a pattern starts to form, since the real solution is to be able to love and approve of yourself, no matter what, and to treat yourself with compassion.

Once you begin to do this, you will not need approval from others and will automatically begin to attract – and be attracted to – people who also treat themselves with compassion and respect.

Part 4 – Mottos to help you fix specific problems

Beware of self-sabotage

Many of us spend a lot of time thinking about what we're looking for in a relationship, and come up with a list of requirements that we believe will make us happy. Although it is great for us to understand what we are looking for in a relationship, there's a danger that we may begin to obsess about what we *think* we want, not what we actually have. We are essentially sabotaging our healthy, balanced, successful relationship. We may tell ourselves that we will only be content if we our partner has certain qualities, and as a result we may refuse to see their other positive qualities. Behaviour is said to be self-sabotaging when it creates problems and interferes with long-standing goals.

The most common self-sabotaging behaviours are procrastination, self-medication (with drugs or alcohol), comfort eating, and forms of self-injury such as cutting. This behaviour can occur at any time, but – regarding a relationship – most often occurs after the honeymoon phase. For example, we may start wondering, 'Is he really the one for me?', 'Is there someone better out there?' or 'This doesn't feel perfect'. These are all self-sabotaging thoughts. While it is natural to have these thoughts, when they descend into obsessive fault-finding we are sabotaging our chance of happiness.

Sometimes we are unaware of what we are doing. However, if you find yourself continuously putting others down or find yourself perpetually angry with your partner, tap into your subconscious and become aware of your motives. If you are behaving like this, then you are blocking your path to a happy relationship.

Once you see that your thoughts and behaviour are forming a negative pattern, then you can start to take steps to change things.

For example, one man in a relationship found it difficult to assertively raise problems with his partner. When she did not behave in the way he wanted, he secretly sought to 'punish' her by ignoring her, staying out late after work, or becoming dismissive. While this at first created the circumstances he wanted – his partner became anxious and focused all her attention on him – over time this proved to be self-sabotage. His partner became fed up with his behaviour and lost respect for him.

This is why awareness of our own behaviour is critical to create healthy ways of relating. Sometimes, this kind of behaviour can be traced to a trigger event, or may be a result of long-standing issues, perhaps (but not always) from childhood.

Either way, once you become aware of it, you can work out why you are behaving in this way. If you don't know the cause, then you cannot properly address your behaviour. In some cases, being honest with yourself will allow you to uncover what drives your actions. In other circumstances, you may need to seek help. Cognitive behavioural therapy (CBT) could help you to do this. It focuses on how your thoughts, beliefs and attitudes affect your feelings and behaviour, and teaches you coping skills.

It can be difficult to remind ourselves that we all deserve love and that it is something we can achieve, if we allow ourselves.

By resolving any negative thoughts, and patterns of behaviour, we open ourselves up to love.

Why money is such a big issue in relationships

What are the main problems regarding money in relationships? Do men and women have different attitudes towards money? Money is a big issue in every aspect of our lives, not just within relationships. We need money to feed ourselves, clothe ourselves, express ourselves, enjoy ourselves, develop ourselves, challenge ourselves, etc. In modern life money talks, and it says a lot about us. How much money you have can therefore have an effect on your self-esteem, self-confidence and self-belief.

If finances are a problem, then you will – understandably – feel concerned, stressed and anxious, and this will inevitably affect your relationship. Many people compare themselves to their peers, then feel inadequate and unsuccessful if they think their peers are achieving more than they are, or doing better than they are.

We naturally want to 'treat' and 'spoil' our partners to show our affection, but how can we do this if we have little money? If the means by which we can do this are restricted, it is almost as though our ability to share our care and affection is also constrained.

The traditional dynamic of 'man as breadwinner, woman as homemaker' can be traced way back in our evolutionary history to when hunter-gatherer males provided for the nurturing, 'motherly' females. By providing well for their female partners, men guaranteed the increased health and success of their offspring, which in turn increased the chance that their genes would be passed on to the next generation. We are still inclined today (no matter how subconsciously) to follow this path. Therefore if a woman feels that her partner is not providing well for her, she may not feel that she is receiving everything necessary to guarantee the health and 'success' of her family, and she may wish to seek support from another partner. It is therefore easy to understand that, if a man feels that he is not providing well for his partner, he will feel concerned, anxious and distressed, and almost as though he is not a 'real man' (because a 'real man's' job is to provide well for his partner and family). Incidentally, finances are frequently cited as a contributory factor in divorce cases worldwide.

If you understand our evolutionary history, it is also easier to see why having a relationship with a more 'powerful' and financially successful woman may be problematic for some men.

Male and female attitudes towards money can also be understood in the context of evolutionary psychology. A man tends to regards wealth as something he should demonstrate (so that he can display his worthiness as a potential partner and mate) whereas a woman may regard wealth as something she can use to provide well for herself and her family. This helps to explain why men tend to be more inclined to purchase 'status symbols' such as expensive cars (particularly during a mid-life crisis, when they are becoming less physically attractive to the opposite sex).

Of course, there are many examples of successful relationships in which the woman is the higher earner and this works perfectly for both parties.

An important part of overcoming any financial tension in relationships is trust: when two people are honest and open with each other, any insecurities about money, success or power are dispelled. If you and your partner argue about money, you need to have a frank, open conversation about it.

Is one partner intimidated by how much the other earns? Are the traditional roles reversed, thus causing the man to feel emasculated?

Is the party who has less money taking advantage of the person with more money? Once you have got to the root of the problem, be compassionate and empathise with your partner. From there, discuss how to resolve the problem or find a joint new perspective on it.

Money is just one area of a relationship. If one partner has less money than the other, what about all the other factors that they bring to the relationship? If one partner has started to take the other for granted, agree what each will contribute and then stick to what you decide. Many relationships fail because couples are too embarrassed to discuss money and simply hope the problem will go away or resolve itself. Don't let this happen to you.

Economic crises and relationships

When a country is in economic crisis, there is often an increase in relationship breakdowns – but, on the other hand, there is also an increase in new marriages! This shows that people can be stressed by the crisis, which is manifested in their relationship, but also that some others remain hopeful and optimistic about relationships and the future.

Today, people may be faced with a host of job-related problems, such as a lack of job security, high unemployment, and zero-hours contracts. This puts a strain on relationships and creates new challenges for couples to deal with. First and foremost, those who rise to this challenge need to recognise that relationships are about working as a team, communication, and of course intimacy...

One factor that may prove challenging to any relationship is increased levels of stress. If you've lost your job, or are at risk of losing your job, so you feel the need to work harder to ensure your place in the company, you will be stressed.

Such an increase in stress and anxiety may put you at risk of becoming clinically depressed, and may change the way you behave. You may become snappy, short-tempered or irritable.

To overcome this, it is important that couples see themselves as a team, and try to overcome any problems together rather than as individuals. It may be helpful if you sit down and talk openly about how you are feeling and what you can do together to help.

Feeling stressed can be tiring. If you're having to work harder to impress your boss, this may mean you have less quality time to spend with loved ones, particularly in the bedroom department.

If you are stressed, you feel less desire. Intimacy is an essential part of a relationship. Research has suggested that cuddles, touches and kisses – as well as sex – make you feel positive and closer to your partner, and make your bond stronger, so it is crucial that you make time to spend with your partner.

Research suggests there is a strong link between job loss/unemployment and poorer physical and emotional health, therefore it is important to support your partner through such times, and also accept their help when needed. Women are often better at dealing with unemployment than men, as they are better communicators. Additionally, a woman's identity tends to be related to a multitude of factors, such as their family life, social life and image, whereas men are more likely to define themselves in terms of their career.

Differing spending habits may also prove challenging during an economic crisis. Most people do not usually take into account their spending habits, and how they value money, when thinking about their compatibility with a partner, as they may not see this as a potential problem – until faced by an economic crisis.

Try to understand that things that may seem insignificant to you may be very serious to your other half. Review your monthly spending together, but do not let it turn into an argument. Perhaps you can come up with new ideas for saving money together, and think about how to stop financial problems becoming any worse. Where could you make economies? Do you need a massage every week? Do you need that expensive gym membership? Try to compromise and come up with alternatives.

It may also be a good idea to review your dreams and goals together, or delay them for a little longer: is it really necessary to invite 300 people to your wedding? Economic crises could also lead to another problem: role confusion. Men have evolved to think they need to be the breadwinner, to protect and provide for their family. They think they are perceived as more desirable when they can display their wealth.

So when suddenly they're no longer able to do this, they feel confused. They may feel lower self-worth, which can cause stress and make them vulnerable to becoming depressed.

Many job losses are in male-dominated careers, such as banking, finance or property, and many men are too proud to ask for, or accept, help. However, whichever party this happens to in a relationship, the starting point is to be as supportive as possible.

Ensure that your partner knows you understand this is not their fault, and it is a temporary situation that you will get through together.

Encourage them to start searching for a new job. Make them feel needed and wanted: ask for their help and advice in the same way you have always done. Being the only breadwinner in a household can also prove stressful. If you are unemployed, make your partner feel appreciated and try to reduce the financial pressure they are under by economising and by taking on more of the household chores.

For example, if your wife is the only person working, you can cook, clean, take the children to school – try to take as much strain off her as possible. And remember, you can treat your partner without spending money on a present: it is always the thought that counts. You could cook her a nice meal, make her breakfast in bed, or treat her to a relaxing massage or foot rub, for example.

Some post-unemployment relationship breakdowns are simply because someone has chosen the wrong partner, who is more interested in money than the person, and leaves when there is no longer any money. Although there are many negative consequences linked to economic crises, there are also some positive stories. Many people lost jobs which had taken over their lives and made them unhappy: they then had the chance to re-evaluate their career and look for a job that would be less stressful and would make them happier. It can also encourage people to do the same with their lives – and help them realise what is actually important in life. People may also see problems in their lifestyle, and their spending habits. They may realise that the luxury they take for granted is not a necessity, and look for alternatives.

So, if you work together as a couple to get through hard times, you can certainly make your relationship stronger.

Co-dependency

Co-dependency means excessive emotional or psychological reliance on a partner. It is one of the worst problems in a relationship. This pattern may start in childhood if a child's need for love is not satisfied by a parent. The child learns to adapt their behaviour to gain approval from their parent. Since the child is not loved for who they are, faults and all, they never gain a strong sense of self-worth, and they carry these cognitive and behavioural patterns into their adult lives. Their early relationship acts as a blueprint for later relationships.

In co-dependent relationships, each partner needs something from the other. One person, for example, may need approval, and a feeling of love and belonging, while the other may need their partner to support a dysfunctional behaviour or mental state, such as a chaotic lifestyle, alcohol or drug dependence, etc. Each supports the unhealthy needs of the other. This sets up a cycle where the behaviour of each is maintained as each party is getting something they need (however dysfunctional it is) from the relationship, therefore neither party changes as their behaviour is being rewarded. Onlookers may well say, 'Why are they still together?', but it is because both are, in some ways, having their unhealthy needs met.

If you are in a co-dependent relationship, you will accept any extreme behaviour or adapt your behaviour in order to preserve the relationship.

You will compromise, overlook your needs and take negative consequences for your partner because, in your mind, this is better than losing the relationship. For example, one partner in the relationship may be drinking heavily, which leads to neglect and conflict in the relationship. In a healthy relationship, this would be raised and addressed, with the hope and intent of resolving the problem.

However, in a co-dependent relationship, it is more likely that the party who is not drinking puts up with the conflict and not having their needs met, as the overall goal of preserving the relationship at any prices feels more important to them, despite the distress it is causing them.

Often the most mistreated party in a co-dependent relationship is the one who, on some level, feels they deserve poor treatment.

Again, this can usually be traced to childhood relationships or a traumatic event in a previous relationship.

How do you know if you are in a co-dependent relationship? What are the signs to look out for? Have a look at the list below.

- Do you make extreme sacrifices for your partner?

- Do you find yourself desperately clinging to your partner?

- Do you feel you need to rescue your partner, even if that means taking negative consequences for them?

- Do you feel that you always give, give, give? (Support, money, sex – this can take many forms.)

- Is the main emotion you feel in your relationship anxiety?

- Do you keep quiet to avoid an argument?

- Do you feel as though you will put up with almost anything to save the relationship?

- Do you secretly know the relationship is bad for you? You can see your emotional, mental and physical health suffering, but you still stay?

If you recognise these signs, understand that you are in a relationship based on approval and need, not love. This can be difficult to understand: your experience may be that when you show certain behaviours, your reward is love, which is why you stay.

This is why it can feel devastating to contemplate leaving this kind of relationship, however difficult it has become.

But you need to realise that if you *do* leave this relationship, your partner will find someone else to fulfil their needs. Likewise, if you don't address the pattern in yourself, you will not find a healthy, loving relationship. Instead, you're likely to attract the same kind of relationship in future.

Recovering from a co-dependent relationship – healing and finding a healthy partnership

- Get help to understand the relationships of your childhood, and how you gained (or tried to gain) love and approval.
- It's crucial to work on your relationship with yourself, and your self-love, so you build a sense of self-respect and self-worth.

- Work on increasing your self-confidence so that you become self-reliant.
- Create clear boundaries about what you will and won't accept – practise this in every relationship in your life.
- Become aware of the behaviours you are prone to when you are seeking approval, and refocus on approving of yourself.

Co-dependent relationships are complicated, so it is wise to seek advice and support from a professional if you think you may be co-dependent. If you work through your emotional and behavioural difficulties, you will be able to attract and maintain the most healthy relationship you have ever experienced. Take action now, as this is what you deserve.

Men: love and sex

It will probably not be news to you to hear that men and women can think very differently about sex. This can be a source of trouble at any stage in a relationship if it is not understood. As we know, men are generally much more able to separate sex and love than women, who tend to link the two.

I don't wish to generalise here – women can, and do, enjoy purely sexual encounters; they are not just for men! However, even from the earliest stages in a relationship, a woman may fail to see that a man is not necessarily falling in love with her if they are having sex. This can lead to confusion and disillusionment about the relationship. It can therefore be helpful to break down the components of sexual desire and love.

In a purely sexual encounter, sex is almost entirely about self-gratification. It is biologically driven and does not involve feelings.

The emphasis is on having our sexual desire fulfilled. However, sex in the context of a loving relationship calls for more emotional involvement. Therefore, although men can be said to be more sexually driven than women (in general), this does not mean that the two are always separate, but both men and women would probably agree that you can have great sex with love and great love without sex. There is no strict line that separates sex from love – sex can facilitate feelings of love, and love can generate sexual desire.

The difference between men and women with regard to sex and love can be seen in cheating behaviour. When men cheat, it is generally sexually driven, whereas for women, there is usually an emotional pull before sexual desire begins. This is why men often say it's worse when a woman cheats because there is more emotion involved.

Whatever the trends, both men and women recognise this and generally feel more pain if someone has had an affair as a result of falling in love rather than due to physical lust.

This is why one of the first questions the innocent party asks when they find out their partner has had an affair is, 'Aare you in love with him/her?' This also explains why breaking up with someone with whom we've had a deep loving bond is more painful than splitting from someone with whom we have had a more sexually based relationship.

Whatever our capacity to separate sex from love, most people would agree that, however enjoyable it is to have sex without love, it is much more exciting and fulfilling to feel both love and desire for a partner. This is why it is so important to keep working on the sexual side of a relationship: for most people, love without sex is little more than friendship. Sex is what separates friends from lovers. So it's good to understand that sex and love do not necessarily go hand in hand, especially in the initial stages of a relationship, but it is equally important to remember that sex is an essential part of the development and maintenance of love.

Introducing a new partner to your friends and family

Our nearest and dearest often think they know what's best for us. But finding a partner is hard enough, so what do you do when you meet someone new and your loved ones don't approve of your new partner?

Your parents may take an instant dislike to anyone you bring home, simply because they think no one is good enough for you. Friends may disapprove because they don't want to lose their 'partner in crime'.

In many cases, family and friends just need some time to get to know your partner – and like them. In other cases, due to social or cultural reasons, perhaps, nothing you do will make a difference to how your family and friends feel. Take time to reflect on the situation and make sure you feel confident about your choice (whether to stay with your partner or to leave them) and why. It is important to take into account your needs and desires, but also the role of family and friends and your place in the community.

However, you may be in an unhealthy relationship and, because love is blind, fail to notice it or choose to ignore it. Your friends and family may see that your new partner is no good for you, and therefore will not like him. Destructive relationships can result in a myriad of negative consequences: you may lose friends, find you have less interest in things you used to enjoy, or begin negative coping strategies (such as drinking).

This won't go unnoticed by your loved ones – and, because they care about you, they will let you know about it.

When you're in a relationship, you're likely to change your behaviour. This can be a positive changes, such as being more active or sociable. Whether the change is good or bad, it usually causes some anxiety for your loved ones. You have to work out whether their anxiety stems from wanting to preserve their relationship with you, or whether it is because they feel the need to protect you.

Relationships can be very tricky when your loved ones disapprove of your partner. Here are some tips to help in this situation.

- It is necessary to remember that, more often than not, those closest to you will be looking out for your best interests. If your loved ones can give solid reasons why they do not think your partner is right for you (e.g. 'he is controlling' or 'I don't like how she speaks to you'), then it may be worthwhile taking a step back from the situation to see if there is any truth in what they are telling you.

- Introduce your partner to your loved ones gradually. If you have brought home a few different potential partners, your loved ones may not take your relationship seriously. Or they may assume the worst and treat them like previous partners, who may not have been right for you. Bring up your partner in conversation with your family and friends. After a while, they will realise that this person is a valued part of your life and be more accepting when they meet them.

- If your loved ones are openly rude about your partner, sit down with them one to one and ask them why they dislike your partner. Try to reassure them that this person makes you very happy. Loved ones may interfere because they are afraid of losing you and scared of your relationship changing. Make sure you keep in contact with them and set aside some one-on-one time to make them feel valued. However, it is very important that you do this on your own terms: don't let them take advantage of your kindness and sacrifice the time that you should be investing in your relationship.

- We often vent to those closest to us whenever our partner does something wrong, but fail to tell them about all the good things he does. If you are always passing on negative information about your partner, those closest to you will form a very one-sided view of him. Stop focusing on the negative, and start telling people about all the nice things your partner does for you too.

- If all else fails, remember: ignorance can be bliss. When a member of your family or a close friend makes a derogatory comment about your partner, ignore it and change the subject. Make sure that your partner does the same. Soon your loved ones will come to realise that your partner is part of your life and nothing will change that. Once they have realised this, their behaviour should improve.

All close relationships are valuable and need to be nurtured. If you and your partner break up, you will need your friends and family to comfort you. Not all relationships work out, no matter how hard we try.

However, if you're in a healthy relationship and your loved ones know how valuable your partner is to you, they will learn to accept them. They may even grow to like them.

Balancing the power in your relationship

Even with the best intentions, many couples fail to achieve a successful power balance in their relationship. This is where each partner feels that they are significant and influential in the relationship. Psychologists believe that a power imbalance, when one party feels less valued or significant, is driven by three main factors: social norms, psychological dependency, and inequity between personal resources.

Power cut

When one partner is seen as powerful, the other may feel they have to submit to them, particularly if they are financially or emotionally dependent on them.

Feeling powerless can lead to resentment, which is often expressed passive-aggressively, such as by withdrawing emotionally. A relationship can be poisoned by the feelings of loneliness that accompany powerlessness: loneliness can result in one partner seeking attention elsewhere.

However, a healthy power dynamic can be created. It means valuing your partner's attributes and recognising each other's strengths. Remember, being with another person is a choice, so when times are difficult focus on what attracted you to each other in the first place. Power dynamics are also not static.

They are fluid, often dependent on external factors, and may very well change throughout a relationship.

Power in love

When power is equally shared in a relationship, communication is more likely to be direct and effective, which means both partners will feel valued and respected.

It is a virtuous cycle that results in a continuation of the shared power balance. This allows both partners to maintain their own identity alongside their shared identity as a couple. A couple that practises equal power-sharing will be able to deal with conflict and stress more easily. Remember: when power is shared, your relationship is likely to be more powerful.

Shifting power dynamics

The balance of power in a relationship depends on the couple, and can shift over time.

Often social norms play a role here, as some people prefer a more traditional set-up. Some people prefer one half of a couple to take a more powerful or directive role than the other, and this is fine as long as it is negotiated and the role of each is valued by the other. However, to say a relationship should always be 50/50 is naive.

There will always be shifts in relationship power dynamics, and these are largely due to circumstances. If one party is made redundant or loses a loved one, it is natural and necessary that the power should shift to ensure that the vulnerable party is protected. Danger can occur if the vulnerable party perceives this as a loss of power rather than a temporary shift in the dynamic of the relationship. Couples should celebrate the fact that they can balance their relationship – it is a sign of a strong partnership if couples can view themselves as a team whatever the circumstances affecting them. As ever, open communication and awareness of power are the keys to allowing shifting power dynamics to strengthen, rather than weaken, a relationship.

Confession is good for the soul

Human beings are naturally curious. We are all drawn to, and curious about, other couples' confessions and secrets.

At Southbank's Love Festival in London, a 'wall of confessions' allows us an insight into what naughtiness others have been involved in: a married woman's recent lesbian experience with her oldest friend; a man's confession that he is still in love with his ex-wife after being divorced for 21 years; a woman's admission that she secretly meets her partner's brother while her partner is out at football.

We read each handwritten note while we tightly hold our own partner's hand, thankful that our relationships are so stable and honest. But are they? With up to 60% of married people committing adultery,[9] a confession may seem the perfect way to absolve yourself of your sins. But when it comes to confessions in a relationship, is honesty really the best policy? And, if so, will it make your relationship stronger?

---

[9]   At: www.truthaboutdeception.com/cheating-and-infidelity/stats-about-infidelity.html

The building blocks of a relationship are truth and trust, and they are cemented together by communication. No matter what the nature of the confession, remember: relationships cannot work without honesty. Lies, even little white lies, can lead to other problems, creating an unstable, unhappy relationship.

Take, for example, confessing a sexual desire. You may have a fantasy or sexual interest that you want to explore with your partner, but you just can't tell them about it.

This could be an act that is important to your sexual happiness, but you may feel too embarrassed or even guilty to mention it. This is perfectly normal, but it's imperative that couples are completely honest with each other if a relationship is to work over the long term.

Not telling the truth about your desires, and not being open with each other, can push couples apart and can lead to one individual looking elsewhere for the closeness they crave. As long as what you desire is legal and takes place between two consenting adults, it is better to discuss it than to bottle it up.

Your partner may be uncomfortable with your fantasy; if so, discuss this together. However, your partner may also have a fantasy they have been too embarrassed to mention to you. Communication is key in any relationship. It helps couples to move forward, thus making them stronger.

Take also, for example, a confession of cheating. It goes without saying that cheating is not appropriate in any loving relationship, and confessing to cheating may seem like a sure-fire way to ruin your relationship – and your partner's trust in you. This may be the case. However, it is not healthy to live with any kind of deceit in a relationship – for either the cheater or the cheated. If you have been unfaithful, consider speaking to your partner about why you cheated: this may open up a discussion about other important issues in your relationship. Do you both feel fulfilled? Appreciated? Loved? Is there a deeper problem that, because of a lack of truth and honesty, you have not discussed? Cheating is – usually – the result of a larger problem. If you can discuss that larger problem, you can begin to create a stronger, more successful relationship. If the individual who cheated confesses, admits they were wrong and is genuinely remorseful, it can allow you to begin to rebuild trust and restore truth and honesty – although this may be a long process.

Confession leads to a sense of relief, forgiveness and understanding. It allows us to disclose information about our thoughts and feelings which, in turn, leads to better psychological and even physical health.[10]

---

[10] At: http://experimentaltheology.blogspot.co.uk/2008/05/postsecret-part-4-postsecret.html

Experiments on disclosure have identified that confession – even confessions not disclosed to another person, but written down – allows people to experience and externalise their emotions, creating a better sense of self. Better self-awareness can result in a stronger relationship.

In order to truly love, you need to be open to, and risk, being hurt. A confession may break your relationship, but often – for your own conscience and your own mental health – it is necessary.

If you can confess your deepest desires and needs to your partner, it could strengthen your relationship.

Children

Children can be a source of joy in relationships, but they can also be a source of stress. That's why it's essential to talk to your partner about having children – do they want any?

If so, when? If one partner is really opposed to the idea of having children, or to accepting children from a previous relationship, this could cause huge problems.

With regard to having children together, many people are very clear about whether they would like to have children or not, and some people are open to the idea 'if they meet the right person'. This needs to be discussed honestly (and fairly early on in a relationship) to prevent heartache in the months or years to come.

There is also the possibility, when starting a new relationship, that you (or the other person) already has children. Most people are quite clear about whether this is something they would embrace – or not. Although meeting someone special means that we often make compromises, it is helpful to know your own thoughts on this before you are swept away with the emotion of being in a relationship.

Any situation in which children are present or desired in a relationship needs, as always, open communication. For example, pretending to like a partner's children from a previous relationship is difficult to maintain if it is true. It is better to be open and say you are finding it a struggle than to try and please your partner and their child. This opens up a conversation so that you can seek understanding and put in place practical arrangements so that your relationship with the child can grow naturally, rather than feel forced.

Often this leads to a great relationship with the child. Equally, we cannot expect a partner to instantly love a child of ours who is not their biological child – all relationships take time to develop, and the more sensitive and open we are about our feelings in this process, the better.

What impact do children have on a relationship? Children need a lot of time and attention, and this inevitably changes the dynamics of a relationship. This is where negotiation is needed so that all parties have their needs met and you all operate as a team.

This can include deciding how much time to spend together, when you need time to yourself and time as a couple, what activities you would like to do as a family and apart, managing the general household arrangements, etc. Making arrangements that suit everyone is paramount in avoiding resentment, withdrawal and arguments.

So if children are part of your relationship, make sure you discuss this with sensitivity, compassion and respect for everyone involved. Time spent discussing everyone's needs and preferences openly is the key to creating a harmonious family life.

Age differences in a relationship

How do you manage communication in a relationship if there is a sizeable age difference between you? There are many preconceptions regarding age differences in romantic relationships, with many people believing that men prefer to date younger women and women prefer to date older men. In some cases this may be correct. For example, a younger woman may decide to date an older man as she may believe he will provide security for their child. However, when having children is taken out of the equation, it is important to highlight that people may be best suited to someone of their own age.

This is because they have similar life experiences, which enhances communication., and are at similar life stages. It is crucial to consider how closely your values match up with those of your partner, and to understand your goals.

When there is a significant age gap between you and your partner you should have a frank, honest conversation regarding what you both want out of life. As mentioned earlier, a successful relationship is built on having similar life goals, an understanding of what you and your partner need and want out of the relationship, and similar characteristics and interests.

Real love is based on friendship combined with attraction: quite often, friendship grows through familiarity and similarity. This may be more likely with someone who is of a similar age as you.

Nonetheless, age should be a secondary factor when choosing a significant other.

You should focus on seeking a partner who is the best match for you, not fulfilling a preference for a younger (or older) partner. Changes in society's views regarding women earning more money and being financially independent may mean that age difference is less important today, as the traditional roles of the man earning the money and the woman staying at home with the children are not as common as they used to be.

Men and their mates

What impact does a man's friends have on his romantic relationship? You might get on with your partner's friends – or you might not. Your partner might spend hours chatting to his mates about cars and football, or his mates could exert a terrible influence on him, keeping him out drinking until the wee hours. Good mates, though, are more than just drinking pals or fair-weather friends.

They care about, support and encourage your partner, and have his best interests at heart. From a woman's point of view, her partner's friends offer an intriguing perspective on the character of the man she loves.

How men relate to and with each other and their shared experiences can be highly informative: she can find out what has made her partner the person they are and how their personality has been shaped. It puts your partner in a new light, revealing and affirming those qualities for which you love and appreciate them. Your partner's friends have the ability to bring out the best in him, and give him the opportunity to engage in interests and pursuits outside your relationship.

It is crucial to acknowledge and embrace your partner's friends for what they bring to his life. It is in our interests to be the best mate possible in all our relationships so that we can give our utmost to our partner.

After all, a mate also means one of a pair, a counterpart and contemporary, a perfect match and a best buddy.

'I don't love you, but I can't leave you'

Couples stay together because they love each other, right? In an ideal world, yes, but this is not always the case. There are other factors that bind people together – children being the obvious one, but also financial commitments, health issues and even pets.

However, resentment and even hatred can build up when a couple stays together for any other reason than love, and this often leads to explosive anger or other 'symptoms' (such as a partner seeking love elsewhere – which, although understandable, can cause even more distress). What can be done in these circumstances? The first step here is honesty and acknowledgement. If you no longer love each other in a romantic way, this needs to be said. If one partner does not feel the same way and is still in love, this complicates the situation, but it is not in anyone's best interest to pretend that nothing has changed.

Most people would prefer to know the truth, no matter how difficult it is to hear.

The truth is that, no matter how difficult a situation is, there is usually a solution somewhere, although this will usually involve compromise. It's probably most difficult if there are children involved, as a split will inevitably affect them. Many couples choose to stay together because of their children, and if this is what you have decided is the best way forward, it is not for anyone to judge you.

However, sometimes a break is necessary, and this needs to be handled with extreme care and respect for all involved. If a situation is so complicated that it seems impossible, this usually indicates that careful planning and time need to be devoted to the process.

It is important to seek advice from experts to discover the best ways to separate so that the well-being of all is protected.

In financially difficult circumstances it is especially valuable to get advice, as there may well be options you are unaware of.

If you are certain you need to get out of a relationship, but you feel trapped, consider that thousands of people have found themselves in similar circumstances but have been able to find a way forward. The key point to remember is to show respect and consideration when you are making decisions and plans, as it is likely that compromise will be necessary, and therefore pain will be part of the process.

However, pain and confusion are necessary states we have to go through on the road to clarity and resolution, so it is better to be prepared for this. Even if your circumstances look bleak or impossible, it is important that you search your soul to see what options you have if the love really has gone. If an immediate resolution is not possible, you will have to make the best of the current circumstances – which can only be done by agreeing on a strategy with your partner for how you will manage until change can be affected. Most people who have split up will say that time is a great healer: given time, all parties can adjust and find happiness again. The most crucial thing is to be true to yourself, while considering others and being respectful towards the feelings of all concerned.

Do I stay or do I leave?

In a world where physical intimacy is a mere click or swipe away, the lines of infidelity can become blurred. However, most people still hold a conventional idea of infidelity. The range of behaviours most associated with infidelity can vary from secret friendships with a person of the gender you find sexually attractive to physical intimacy. What fidelity means is inevitably different for each person.

There are numerous forms of cheating, such as emotional infidelity (which means your partner having feelings for someone else, or being in love with someone else). They may not have been unfaithful physically. Secret friendships are often the first step on the slippery slope to emotional infidelity. This does not mean that friendships with specific people or specific genders are not allowed; it is about ensuring that your partner's emotional needs in the relationship are not being met by someone else.

You need to set boundaries in your relationship. Communication is key to understanding what infidelity means to you and your partner. There is no use having cheating defined in your mind and not discussing this with your partner, as they may well have a different definition of cheating. You need to establish what behaviours you deem acceptable, for you and for your partner, and you must both be on the same page about fidelity and exclusivity.

For some, a flirtatious display of affection would not be deemed as cheating; for others, it would.

It is also important to ensure you do not slip into a harmful mindset. Jealousy can jeopardise a perfectly happy and successful relationship, leading to a breakdown in trust and communication. You must trust your partner.

Jealousy and believing that your partner has been unfaithful when they have not been can be just as damaging as your partner actually cheating. There's a fine line between being passionate about your relationship and being possessive and jealous.

If you partner cheats on you, it is devastating. Often you will be unable to think of him/her in the same way again. Overcoming this, or making the decision to leave, requires time. Sometimes, however, our hurt feelings may blind us to the strength of the relationship as a whole.

Often a breach of trust results from one area of a relationship in which needs have not been fulfilled, and this can be addressed. Take time to talk – not just to your partner, but to other people you trust. Try to take a rational view and acknowledge how the relationship has reached this point.

If the underlying problem is resolvable, with sensitivity and open communication you may well be able to resolve the issue. However, this is not always the case. If the infidelity has involved months or years of deceit, you may well feel there is no going back and you deserve better. Taking the time to consider your needs is the way forward, whether you choose to remain in the relationship or end it.

Infidelity is a breach of trust. Your partner has behaved in a way that you consider disrespectful and unacceptable. It's up to you to choose how to proceed.

Open, honest communication about the situation and what went wrong can strengthen a relationship – or end it.

Is religion a big deal?

Many people feel the desire to connect with a higher power – such as the supernatural or a particular deity. We gravitate towards the transcendental, the sacred and the divine. Many think of religion in terms of the world religions and their subgroups.

Religion is very subjective: our definition of ourselves is often related to our religion. If we lack knowledge and understanding of others' beliefs, and do not acknowledge their beliefs, prejudice prevails, and people's perceptions of religion can be reduced to broad brushstrokes and crass stereotyping.

Our understanding of different religions may be clouded by the opinions of our family, friends and associates, while what we see and hear in the media can leave us confused.

This can impede our ability to empathise with people from a different religion to our own, to appreciate their beliefs and respect their right to worship. Many social events and family occasions have their basis in a shared religion, and religious doctrine can also reinforce accepted standards regarding marital practices and choice of partner.

Given religion's significance in terms of who we are, how we see ourselves and others, and the decisions we make in our lives, it is unsurprising how much influence religion can have on our selection of a life partner and our relationship with them.

Recently, there has been a tendency for more people to describe themselves as agnostic or spiritual, favouring a less rigid outlook on humankind's connection with the sacred. This way, we can appreciate the religion in the person rather than the person in terms of their religion.

Most people don't wish religion to be the dominant factor in their relationships. That said, the major religions today are for many people a source of contentment, solace and power, enriching the lives of those who follow them and the people they know. Religion gives many people a sense of purpose and direction.

In a world that is increasingly cosmopolitan and where marriage between people of different ethnicities, cultures and religions is ever more common, most people need not decide between their religion and their relationship.

If we abandon our preconceptions, we are more likely to attract people into our lives we never would have met otherwise. Talk to your partner about their religion: use it as a platform from which to share experiences and learn about each other. Religion and relationships are not mutually exclusive but beautifully inclusive: let's give them a chance to work together.

Deciding whether or not to have children

If neither of you have children, this potentially life-changing event is something that needs a great deal of consideration. Ideally, you should discuss parenthood relatively early in a relationship: if you and your partner have different wants in this area, this is likely to lead to heartache and potentially the end of the relationship. There are some key points to consider when thinking about having a child together.

Why do you want a child?

It may seem like an unusual place to start, but it's important to understand why you feel the way you do about having children. We are conditioned from our early years that having children is an expected part of life, but having children is not right for everyone. Also, some women may still feel pressure to have children. However, it is important that your decision to have children is based on what you really want, not society of family expectations. As they age, women may hear the ticking of their biological clock. Even though there are now many different options that allow women to have children much later in life, you still have to consciously consider the prospect of children rather than leave it to chance.

Commitment

The other point to consider is the commitment involved in bringing up children.

Having children means that the next eighteen years of your life, at least, will be occupied by raising them. This may seem obvious but many people have children simply because their peer group are having them, without considering whether this is right for them and their relationship.

Timing and practicalities

Following on from the above point, the timing of parenthood is important. However, this does not necessarily mean that you can time conception, obviously! However, thinking about the career paths of both partners, as well as other existing commitments, can help you decide when the time might be right to have children.

What happens if you want children but your partner doesn't?

When it comes to deciding whether to become a parent, it is perfectly all right to make any decision, and no one should judge you either way. A difficulty arises when one person wants children but their partner doesn't. The first step here is to establish whether this is 'no for now' or 'never'.

If they have truly opposing views about whether or not to have children, this could be a threat to the relationship. This is why you should discuss parenthood early on in a relationship, to avoid potential heartache later. Both parties need to talk openly and honestly about their vision of the future and see whether they can come to an agreement.

It should go without saying that a couple should never have a child if the relationship is in difficulty, or to try to 'save' a relationship. If you both decide to have children, you should see the decision as an exciting, life-enhancing commitment.

Becoming a step-parent

Going from being a single person to being a step-parent involves a huge change to identity. This can be an exciting time, but may also be a time of anxiety.

In either case, becoming a step-parent usually brings challenges, and it's helpful to be prepared for these challenges from the outset.

Here are some guidelines.

The first point to consider is that the child or children may still be hurt and angry about their parents breaking up. They may feel resentful or jealous towards the step-parent and blame them (even if you met your partner long after they split up with their ex). The welfare of the child should obviously be central, and needs to be handled with sensitivity. It is important to tread carefully, acknowledge that the child may not accept you at first, and show respect for the child's emotions and behaviour, which may be accepting and welcoming or may be hostile.

Continue to reach out sensitively even if the child dismisses you.

Explain your role to the child. Tell them you are not there to replace their mother or in any way change their relationship with their father.

This can be comforting for the child, who may well be confused about the new roles developing within the family. Initially approach a relationship with a step-child as if you are making a new friend. Never project your needs on to the child – you may feel the need for their approval and love, but you should discuss your feeling with your partner. They should not impact on the child.

Go out with your step-child so that you can have fun together and get to know them better – and vice versa. Having fun going to the cinema, bowling or to the park can help them get used to the new family situation.

Move slowly. The more you force the relationship, the more it will elude you. Children can sense pressure and will know that the adults around them will want everyone in the family to get on.

The less pressure you put on the child, and the more you allow the relationship to grow of its own accord (as you would with any other friendship), the better your chances of having a great relationship for the long term.

Establish a support network for yourself. Obviously your first point of support and communication should be your partner, and you should be honest about your feelings, concerns and triumphs. However, you may need more than just your partner. Having supportive friends or family can help you handle the challenges a step-child can bring, and can also ensure you retain your sense of identity as yourself as well as part of a new family.

Introducing your child to your new partner

What about if you have a child or children and your new partner doesn't? The above guidelines are relevant for this scenario as well, but there are further points to consider if you are introducing your child to a new partner.

Your child may have a range of feelings about you having a new partner, but never make assumptions about how your child is feeling. Talk to your child. Are they feeling threatened? Jealous? Resentful? Bitter? Hurt? They may feel overwhelmed. The key thing to do is to validate their feelings – let them know it's fine for them to feel whatever they want (even if you wish they didn't). The only way your child will be honest with you about their feelings is if they do not feel reproached for their honesty, so if you want the truth, you have to be good at hearing it.

Spend time alone with your child. This will show the child that you love them and value them, and that this will not change. If your child feels secure in their relationship with you, they are more likely to be happier and settled. If the child does not feel secure about their relationship with you, they will react negatively to anyone they see as a threat to that relationship.

The above guidelines also apply for introducing your child to a new partner – take the relationship slowly, do not put any pressure on the child, and keep talking to your child. Build in some fun activities you can all do together – this may be easier than making conversation over a meal, which children can find uncomfortable in the early days.

Dating when you both have children

There are opportunities for joy and for challenges when both parties have children from a previous relationship.

This can often be a great starting point for a relationship and new family as both partners appreciate the demands of being a parent. However, there is the additional challenge of how best to blend your families. Here's how to manage this situation.

Each parent needs to talk openly with their child or children about their new partner. As with the guidelines above, communication is everything. Ask your child how they feel about the situation. Validate their concerns and say that they are always allowed to be open with you about how they feel as they meet your new partner and children.

When you first introduce your child to your new partner and their children, a neutral place is the best venue – somewhere the children will enjoy, and where there's lots to do and see, to give you all something to talk about.

Allow the children to find their own way to communicate and bond without pressure. There may well be conflict between children, and you will need to handle this carefully and in an unbiased way. Try not to favour your child.

Maintain a united front with the children. Children may well test boundaries in this situation and play one parent off against the other. While it is natural for children to do this, it is important that both partners show a united front so they don't confuse the child. If you don't do this, there is likely to be more conflict in the long term for all involved, so communicate with your partner about how you will handle certain situations in advance, as far as possible.

The most important thing here is to think of the welfare of everyone concerned. Be sensitive to the needs of the children and to both parties in the relationship.

As with all areas of a relationship, open communication is the key to problem-solving and building strong and meaningful relationships.

Stress over Christmas

Psychologists have noted that most people who get stressed over the festive period fail to recognise or acknowledge it, putting it down to tiredness or hangovers. Christmas means spending more money than usual, catering for many people, spending time with in-laws, guests and extended family, attending work Christmas parties, and the expectation that everything will be perfect. It's no surprise that this leads to stress.

Causes of stress

The two weeks before Christmas is one of the peak times for couples to break up. Christmas is infamous for bringing to the surface the little cracks in relationships.

It's important to understand the causes of stress before finding out how to reduce or manage them, ensuring your relationship stays strong over the Christmas period and into the New Year.

Expectations: whether these are the expectations of children, wanting that 'must have' toy, or the expectations of family, friends and partners, it's important to be realistic. Don't try to achieve the impossible. Also, remember to include your partner. If you are attending events together, or a family event, make sure you do not leave them out or exclude them in conversations – it is easy to be complacent with the people we love the most.

'Our Christmas': The term 'our' is central here. 'In our house we do this...' If you are a new couple, merging the traditions you are both used to can cause stress for both of you.

Logistics: We are expected to spend time with our own family and our partner's family. If your families do not live close to one another, trying to visit everyone within a short space of time can be stressful.

Patience: Stress is often caused when a loved one runs out of patience. With added pressure, we often become short and snappy. If you see this happening, make sure you acknowledge and recognise it and apologise.

Role reversal: When we visit our parents, we tend to revert to being a child again. Psychologists have noted this phenomenon! It is important to acknowledge how your partner might perceive this role shift, as it may make them feel uncomfortable, especially if you do not visit your parents often. This will cause stress for you and your partner.

How to manage seasonal stress

Make time for the following:

Each other: Making time for your partner is essential. Although you and your partner will be jointly attending all the festivities, in the Christmas rush it is easy to forget to spend time alone with your partner.

Make a few dates where you will spend time alone together to stay connected. Visit a Christmas market, or attend the ballet or a theatre production – do whatever you enjoy as a couple, but make time for one other.

Communication: This is key. Speaking to each other will help maintain your romantic bond. If you feel your partner is being unrealistic, for example about how many social engagements you can both attend during the Christmas period, speak to them about your concerns and tell them what is important to you. Take a step back and look at your own behaviour – we often see ourselves as being right all the time, but try to see things from your partner's perspective. If an apology is in order, say sorry.

Being united: The way you do Christmas changes when you're in a relationship. Create your own traditions, recognising what's important to both of you from your childhood or past that you both want to continue.

Helping each other: Often, when your partner is stressed, it is easy to offer them advice. Be careful here, because this may look as if you think you can handle the situation better than they can, which may make them feel inadequate. Instead, offer a compassionate ear. Affection, which releases the love hormone oxytocin, also helps to reduce stress, so cuddling your partner will help lift their mood.

Create a plan: Prearranging when you will see each other's family, shop, organise, prepare and even tidy for Christmas will help you to manage each other's expectations and those of others.

Time: Give yourself enough time to complete mundane tasks as well as the things you will enjoy together. Avoid leaving things to the last minute, so you can have extra time with your partner instead of wrapping emergency gifts.

Although Christmas can be the most wonderful time of the year, it can also be stressful, especially if you're doing lots of entertaining.

Taking notice of each other's feelings and appreciating the contribution that you are each making over Christmas will ensure you both feel special and cared for, allowing you both to enjoy the festivities.

Part 5 – Mottos to help you invest in yourself and your relationship

Keep working on your self-esteem

We develop self-esteem though positive life experiences: as young children, through our relationships with family members and teachers; at school, through academic achievements and social inclusion.

We compare ourselves to others and assess our worth. Receiving positive reinforcement when we have done something well, or for being funny, intelligent or good-looking, can help boost our self-esteem.

However, not doing well, and feeling unpopular or being bullied, can lower our self-esteem. People with healthy self-esteem tend to have firm beliefs and values, but are open to different views and secure enough to change their mind and acknowledge when they are wrong. They also have the best relationships.

Good self-esteem can come from the satisfaction of doing something well. When you are feeling low about yourself, it might be because there is something you could be doing better. Rather than sinking into depression, acknowledge your feelings and allow them to motivate you to focus on improving whatever you feel low about. Healthy self-esteem is vital to maintain a healthy relationship.

How do we create great self-esteem?

What you can do each day

Monitor your thoughts – don't let yourself talk negatively. Your unconscious mind is always paying attention to what you say. Even if you are soothing yourself by saying 'I don't need to feel nervous about talking to my partner', you are heightening your awareness of the fact that you're feeling nervous in the first place. So think as positively as you can. Try saying to yourself instead, 'This conversation will be a good learning experience.' It works much better. Leave self-deprecation to other people – being negative about yourself or your relationship may make others laugh, but it's not the best approach in terms of strengthening self-confidence.

What you can do each week

Make time to visualise what you want out of life and your relationships. You may be dreaming of marriage, or rekindling a lacklustre relationship, or something else entirely. Spend time visualising your goal and watch yourself living that goal on a movie screen inside your head (as though it has already happened). By doing this, you will become more familiar with what you seek.

Research has shown that the more we identify with our goals, and the more detail we give them, the more likely we are to achieve them.

What you can do each month

Reward yourself – everyone responds well to rewards! However, rewarding yourself randomly, while it may be fun, does not work. Think about when you should treat yourself and your relationship. Reward yourself only when you have done something positive towards your goal or tried very hard at something. Be honest with yourself and give yourself genuine positive encouragement as you strive to reach your goals. Be sure to find a reward that works for you or, if it's a relationship goal, a joint reward. Even a small reward, such as saying something nice to yourself, works – it costs nothing and makes you feel good.

What you can do each year

Review old goals and set new ones. Goal-setting is great when we set goals that we genuinely want: goals that are realistic, positive and meaningful. Setting meaningful goals is something everyone should do regularly. Why? Because goals focus our attention and direct our efforts (and, when tied in with a reward, research shows that we become much more persistent, too). However, it is crucial to set realistic goals that are achievable. The goal should be within your control.

If you are feeling low about yourself, you might have negative thoughts, such as 'My partner does not love me enough'. People with high self-esteem, on the other hand, are likely to focus on the positive aspects of themselves. This means they are more likely to inject positivity into the relationship, generating a higher sense of commitment from both partners and increasing their overall well-being.

Changing the way that you see things will also affect how others see you, causing a virtuous cycle rather than the destructive one you may be stuck in now. For example, thinking 'He no longer loves me' or 'I'm not attractive enough' will result in negative, closed-off body language that will stop your partner wanting to approach you. Thinking 'I am attractive' and 'We are building a great relationship', and smiling, will do the opposite.

Why do women check out other women?

We all like to compare ourselves to others. Women will take every opportunity to look at 'real' women. In fact, women are more likely to check out other women than they are to check out men. This is because there's so much pressure on women to look good. Women check each other out because they need to feel good about themselves, they may want something to aspire to, or they may seek a reference point to see if they fit in. This can be on a conscious or subconscious level.

In general, do women look at other women in a positive or negative light? Women are more likely to compliment each other than make a catty remark. Women generally look at physical features they think are important, such as clothes, hairstyle, tan, size, body shape, cleavage, hair colour, bust size, shoes and bag, and the presence or absence of cellulite. These are symbols of social success.

Women tend to engage in a lot of upward comparison, comparing themselves to people they perceive as better off. Women also have a tendency to judge themselves harshly. There's no point in most women comparing themselves to a supermodel. That will not end well. It's perfectly normal and healthy to compare yourself to others.

However, when your ideals become unrealistic and unachievable this makes you feel bad about yourself.

Women have become much more image conscious in recent years, and who could blame them? It's natural to care about your appearance: after all, looking good has been shown to have evolutionary advantages. Images of women in the media are often blamed for making women feel bad about themselves, as normal women cannot compete with the air-brushed photographs seen in magazines.

Additionally, we live in a world where everyone has a camera phone, and photos are instantly uploaded for the world to see. This potentially adds to the pressure women feel to look good always.

Why do women compliment other women? Women tend to feel comfortable doing this. They use complimentary language as a way to build a rapport with someone.

Complimenting someone could be seen as a way to place yourself in a similar category as the person you are complimenting. You have the same bag? You have the same taste. You are therefore in the same social group. You belong. Plus, by giving a compliment, you are giving your approval and thus you gain social advantage, because your opinion matters.

But what if you become obsessed with comparing yourself to other women? Try to check in with yourself rather than constantly checking out others. Think about why you constantly look at other women, and how that makes you feel about yourself. Remember that you should want to look good for yourself, and that no one's perfect. It might be helpful to spend some time focusing on your inner qualities to take the focus off your physical appearance.

Do men check out other men? And, if so, is it carried out in the same way? Like women, men also check each other out. However, while women are more likely to check out other women than they are to check out men, men are more likely to check out women. They look at other men much less often. There is also pressure on men today to look good and to have a good body.

How to maintain good mental health

Most people would benefit from applying psychology to different situations in their life. The good news is that you don't need to be a psychologist to benefit from it – anyone can use it. Psychology can help you better understand your family and friendships, work, relationships and feelings around intimacy. Here are just a few ways you can benefit from using psychology in your life.

Deal with sensitive people more effectively

Many people are sensitive – maybe you have colleagues, friends or family who are sensitive, or perhaps your partner is a sensitive soul. Such people feel things acutely and react quickly and deeply to situations. This can be difficult both for them and for others, so what can you do to understand and communicate with sensitive people?

When working with a sensitive person or partner, you should avoid using negative language. Rather than saying 'Don't worry', try saying 'Stay calm – everything is under control.' This is because the use of negative words can lead too-sensitive people to feeling more upset. Did you know that, when we hear a sentence, we process the word we hear last? When telling someone, 'Don't worry,' the first word they will process is 'worry', and the word 'don't' will come last, when they've already started to worry.

Identify stressors and how to cope with them

While small doses of stress can be good for us, long-term stress can be harmful and lead to ill-health. The main stressors in life are those we feel we have little or no control over. Psychologists have observed that people who feel a problem is out of their hands are likely to have a more intense emotional and physiological reaction to it. When faced with a situation in which we feel we are losing control, the best option is to adopt an appropriate, result-focused, coping strategy. For example, you may be experiencing problems with introducing your children to your new partner, and feel your children's emotional reaction will be out of your hands.

A way to overcome this is to take a proactive approach. Seek advice from people who have been in similar situations, and ask how they handled it.

If you do not know anyone who has been in this situation, speak to an expert or friend, or try easing your children in to the new situation. Ask your children how they would feel about meeting your new partner, and tell your children as much about them as possible before introducing them. Also, make sure you spend plenty of time with your children, so they don't feel that your new partner is taking you away from them. Unfortunately, we cannot always take control of every situation: for example, the death of a loved one. The best we can do is find ways to cope with our emotions.

Check in with yourself and your partner
Sometimes it's good to check in on where you are now, where you would like to be, and how you plan on getting there. Only you can make sure that you are your best possible self.

Additionally, you need to check in with your partner frequently. This is the best way of preventing problems.

Try writing about your future vision for the relationship and for yourself. This will help you to create a logical structure for the future and can turn your abstract ideas into concrete possibilities. Note the strengths of your future self and any changes you will need to make now in order to turn your vision into reality. Take a few minutes every day to remind yourself of this vision. Keep it fresh in your mind and remember that you can achieve it if you wish to.

When things go wrong – we all have bad days – it's easy to become focused on the negative and lose motivation. Visualising your best possible self can help you to re-establish your priorities in life.

As you imagine your goals in life, you will also find ways to overcome obstacles.

Today is the start of a new chapter in your life. Focusing on the positive things to come, and putting the past behind you, can be very therapeutic.

Make the most of your support network

Have you ever wondered why people are often so protective of their family? Even when relationships between family members are strained, family members usually come together to help and protect each other any way they can. According to evolutionary psychologists, we are protective of family members (in many instances, regardless of the situation) because kin selection enables us to look after a common gene pool. This has been used to explain a variety of altruistic behaviours and also to explain why a high percentage of relationships break down because one person dislikes the other's family or family members (such as their children).

Capitalise on the natural support network of your family – they are already motivated to look after your best interests.

Create a fulfilling relationship

Choosing to commit to a lifelong partner can be difficult. Evolutionary psychologists have suggested that, when selecting a partner, men and women look for different qualities than they possess, to ensure a more balanced relationship.

However, we are more than just biological vehicles for our genes. Understanding psychology helps us to understand the broader picture: background, value systems, relationship goals and lifestyle goals are just as vital as chemistry in terms of longevity in a relationship. Take the time to use the mottos and insights in this book to create a relationship that is truly meaningful.

Self-image, confidence and success

Is image as important as personality?

To answer this question, let's think about how a relationship starts. We meet someone to whom we are attracted in some way; we have great chemistry with them; we build a connection; that connection becomes a bond; the chemistry become less explosive and more stable as the bond is cemented. Image plays a significant role in igniting the fire for most people: it may not be as important as personality, but it is the gateway. We initially assess someone's appearance to give us clues to someone's deeper character. Image may also play a part, in the long term, in keeping that flame burning. Our image is a reflection of our personality and values. A change in our image suggests changes in other factors, and could raise alarm bells in a relationship. Image is very powerful. It should not be confused with looks: image is how we present ourselves – what we choose to wear, how we style our hair, the shoes we wear, the brands we wear. At the same time, image is not everything; nothing is more alluring than a genuinely charming and charismatic personality.

How do you use psychology to understand what cements an individual to another?

The physical elements of attraction are actually only a small part of one's overall attractiveness and (as mentioned earlier), what men find attractive can be different to what women find attractive. In addition to how we present ourselves, much of a man's attractiveness comes from his charisma, confidence, aura of power/success, charm (and how he makes others around him feel), manners, and the way he holds himself, walks and talks. Much of a woman's attractiveness comes from her femininity, her general and emotional intelligence, her positive attitude and her warmth.

How do people make mistakes with their image?

By social comparison: we may evaluate ourselves based on other similar people around us; this may be upwards or downwards. Downward comparison helps us gain self-regard while upward comparison reduces self-regard. We probably do the latter more often, to make us strive to be better. When it comes to our image, there is a huge amount of social comparison taking place, otherwise how would we know how to present ourselves appropriately? However, with image, different things work for different people. Sometimes people get their image wrong because they are trying too hard, and attempt to follow what is on trend rather than dressing for their body type and personality. If you feel uncomfortable in a dress, you probably look uncomfortable. It is also true that sometimes there is a disconnect between how we see ourselves and how others see us.

Some people struggle to put together an outfit; they take everything out of their wardrobe, finally settling on an outfit they hope looks good. Some people claim not to care about the image they present. Not blindly following fashion is a statement of individuality.

Image is important as it is a manifestation of how we feel on the inside. This is why, in relationships, changes in image can signify that we are getting too comfortable, losing interest or going through a difficult time with something. However, maintaining an attractive image for our partners is respectful – after all, in the beginning both sexes think carefully about what to wear for each other and spend lots of time grooming. Letting this slip as time goes by can indicate we have lost respect for our partner. Staying attractive and making an effort is something both parties should continue, as it reinforces self-esteem and the positive energy within a relationship.

How to adopt a positive mindset

We all know the benefits of becoming more positive, and every self-help book advocates a positive mindset, but how do we achieve this and apply it in our relationships?

1. *Find a way to motivate yourself.* What makes you feel happy? Find a way to incorporate this into your day.

2. *See the funny side of life.* When in a stressful situation, try to take a moment to stop and reflect. What is the funny side of this situation?

3. *Manage stress better.* Exercise is one of the best ways to combat stress and raise your happiness levels. If the gym isn't your scene, why not try something different, such as laughter yoga? You could think about exercising with your partner.

4. *Make a 'positive' list.* Write a list of all the things in your life that are positive and make sure that you can see the list where you tend to be most stressed, such as at work. Also make a list of the positive things about your relationship.

5. *Treat yourself.* Make regular time for yourself where you can relax and enjoy yourself, whether it is a spot of retail therapy, meeting up with friends or a picnic in the park for one. Block this time out in your diary, if you have to. This will help you to realise that you are important too. It will also help your relationship if you have some quality time to yourself.

6. *Explore your mind.* Taking some time to explore your feelings is a great way to centre yourself when you feel stressed or

down. For example, reflect on what is making you stressed: do you only feel stressed in certain situations or around certain people? Keep a diary in which you note down events and your feelings in relation to them: this may be a good first step to identifying any changes you could make in your life that would make you happier. This will improve communication in your relationship – you need to know yourself first.

7. *Surround yourself by happy people.* If you are surrounded by happy, positive people then this is likely to affect your mindset, and make you happier as well. Make sure you socialise with your partner and with people who make you both feel uplifted.

8. *Focus on your own life.* Stay focused on your own goals and on what you want from life. Avoid comparing yourself to others. There will always be someone who is financially or socially more successful than you are. Next time you start to compare yourself, try thinking of it this way – every minute you spend thinking about someone else is less time you have to spend on your own life and success.

9. *Increase your positive thoughts.* Notice when you are having negative thoughts and try to think of two positive thoughts to counteract each negative one. Retrain your brain and thought patterns so they work for you rather than against you. Take control of your mind!

10. *Make time to play.* Even adults can benefit from making time to play, whether this is with friends, your children or a partner. Incorporating more playfulness into your life and relationship increases the amount you laugh with the people who are special to you, which can improve your relationships with them.

11. *Increase physical touch in your intimate relationships.* Studies have shown that physical contact, such as hugging and kissing, has physiological benefits and can improve psychological well-being.

Create a vision of your future

Most of us have no qualms about investing in our friends, family, children or careers. We will invest in our companies, our employees, our properties and our finances, but for some reason we are not so good at investing in ourselves. Investing in ourselves is about more than just devoting time to ourselves – investing in our relationship is also the key to relationship success. The most neglected area of 'us' is usually related to our emotional and psychological well-being and self-esteem.

Many people today are working harder than ever to keep their current job or business alive, but the time this takes leaves other areas of their life wanting. Of course, we only have so many resources as human beings, and to a certain extent some imbalance is inevitable, but people who choose to invest some time and energy in themselves and their self-esteem will find it much easier to deal with tough times.

We are constantly told to invest in property, in the stock market or in a pension, yet the best, longest-lasting investment we can make is in ourselves and our relationship.

Regardless of the area of your life you feel needs the most focus, personal development and growth come from goal-setting, actions that help achieve this, and positive thinking.

Our values are the reasons behind our life choices and, in any relationship, shared values are the key to longevity. Yet many of us do not even know what some of our most fundamental values are. To understand more about your core values, try the following exercise. Decide how important to you each of the values below are, and rate them on a scale of 1–3 (with 1 being extremely important):

- Health

- Appearance

- Friendship

- Social life

- A variety of interests and activities

- Marriage

- Having children

- A stable relationship

- A passionate relationship

- Ability to devote time to family/children

- Freedom and independence

- A fulfilling career

- Being financially comfortable

- Independence

- Creativity

- The freedom to create, change and choose my own lifestyle

- House ownership

- Spirituality and religion

- To contribute to my community or to charity – the greater good

- To be remembered for my accomplishments

- Helping those in distress

- Enough leisure time

- A stable life

- Solitude

- Roots in the place I live

Then ask your partner to do the same. Now, take a look at the values you have both rated as being extremely important. These are the things you will never be fully happy without. See how your values correspond with your partner's. This can help you to understand the differences between you. You and your partner do not have to share all the same values, or the same timeframe (for example, your partner may also want children, but they may want to focus on another area of life first), but it is essential that your partner has *similar* values to you, so you can live together and be happy.

The End

"When one loves somebody everything is clear; where to go, what to do – it all takes care of itself and one doesn't have to ask anybody about anything."
Maxim Gorky

We hope you enjoyed reading this book, and we wish you every success in keeping your love blooming.

Made in the USA
Columbia, SC
14 September 2018